WHEN STRONG WOMEN CRY

Oheneyere Gifty Anti

Contact the Author
Tel: 0203535500/ 0543618182
Email: gdaconcepts@gmail.com

Praise for the book

As an ardent advocate of feminism, and as a woman and mother, I know that sometimes the strongest women are the ones who love beyond all mistakes/faults, weep behind closed doors, and engage in battles that nobody knows about. But, it will be a mistake if anyone thinks women cry because they are weak. It's an outburst of pent-up emotions. It's worth noting that a strong woman loves who she is, trusts her instincts, and speaks her mind. This book, authored by the venerable Dr. Gifty Anti (Oheneyere) like its author, is innovative, impactful, clear, and able to open pathways to new ideas. It should not be a "women's only read", no! I recommend it to everyone. Read and you shall never regret it.

—Oheneyere Esi Antwi Bosiako.
President/CEO, Omama Services Incorporated,
Wolcester, Massachusetts. U. S. A

From the grassroots level through to international spheres, Oheneyere Gifty Anti has carved a niche for herself. Her selfless involvement and conscious efforts at raising and maintaining living standards for children and women in deprived communities are spectacular. Having experienced decades of what life may bring, Gifty has now become a large shoulder that the small and the great find to cry on. She is seen and known as a strong woman. Strong women cry too but on whose shoulder and in what circumstance are they allowed to cry?

My encounter with Gifty Anti happened in London, United Kingdom in the year 2022 which revealed her innermost being during our maiden women's conference.

'When Strong Women Cry' authored by Oheneyere Gifty Anti is one of her latest books which you must read to pull yourself through endeavors in life without failing. This book is safe to read as it draws on personal experiences and opens one's eye to the realities of climbing heights in life.

—Reverend Dr. Evelyn Beulah Annan.

Dedication

This book is dedicated to all strong women. May they not only cry in the rain and shower but cry freely because it ok to".

A strong woman is a woman who stands up for herself, regardless.

> *"She is not afraid to share her ideas and thoughts, regardless of what others think. She speaks her heart and her mind. She respects herself enough to stand up for herself, the causes she believes in and the welfare of others"*—Unknown

In the Bible, we can talk about Abigail, Naomi, Ruth, Esther, Deborah, Dorcas and many others.

In the Qu'run, we can talk about Asiya, wife of Pharaoh, Khadija wife of Prophet Mohammed, (peace be upon his name) and Fatima, daughter of the Prophet and Khadija.

In history, we can talk about Nana Yaa Asantewaa of Ghana, Huda Sha'arawi of Egypt, Funmilayo Ransome-Kuti of Nigeria, Zenzi Miriam Makeba of South Africa, etc.

I am sure all these women had stories that made them cry.

There are also women in our time—in this 21st century, who have or have had their own reasons to cry. In this book, I share the beautiful stories of their strength and triumphant through their circumstances.

Acknowledgement

"There is this belief that a strong woman must not appear vulnerable. She must not show any weakness or brokenness. I disagree."
—Oheneyere Gifty Anti

"I invited you here because I have followed you on social media. I read what you write. I learn from and appreciate you all. But I feel I need to share with you certain things that you must watch out for on this feminism/gender advocacy/activism journey. You all know it can be very lonely; the terrain makes it important for you to appear strong. Today I want to be vulnerable before you all so you can perhaps, better understand the pitfalls, when they come. My dear ladies, I have been through some xyz times (I held nothing back, because they are my daughters), lately and I want to share with you so you will feel free to share with me anytime you feel vulnerable and don't know who to turn to because this journey can be very lonely"..

This was my opening statement to my 10 feminist "daughters". I had invited them to my office for a detox session. It was Friday, 10th March, 2023.

We had a good session. We talked, ate kenkey and grills and laughed our lungs out. They all gave me good feedback when they got home. But Eugenia Boadi sent me this message:

"New book title:
Strong Women do Cry
The Detox Formula for Feminists.
Authors: Mama and her avengers"

This gave me the "aha moment". So to the 10: Bashiratu Kamal-Muslim, Felicity Nelson, Babiee Dappah, Nana Akosua Hanson, Jayjay Akuamoah, Juliana Ama Kplorfia, Affi Agbenyo, Francisca Nancy Hagan, Eugenia Boadi and Evangeline Osabutey... who came when Mama called. #MamasAvengers hahaha.

Thank you.

I hope you now understand that it is only natural that strong women, yourselves included—the strong young women, also cry. No, we don't always have to cry in the rain. We can create the space for us to cry openly, too. And I promise to be that woman you can trust and have that safe crying space with.

I will also like to say THANK YOU TO:

- Nana Afrakoma II - Paramount Queenmother of Akwamu Traditional Area
- Dr. Angela Dwamena Aboagye - CEO, The Ark Foundation
- Honourable Abla Dzifa Gomashie, MP for Ketu South
- Mrs. Mary Amoah - CEO, Klicks Africa
- Juliana Ama Kplofia - Feminist/Activist
- Franka Nancy Hagan - Feminist/ Activist
- Justina Yiadom-Boakye - Founder & President, Osteogenesis Imperfecta Foundation Ghana
- Gloria Abla Pwamang - Cosmetologist
- Ms. Maxine Kyeiwaa Sencherey (Kyei Wizzy) - Hotelier and Entreprenuer
- Mrs Mercy Osei-Ghansah - Educationist and Entreprenuer

And all those who chose to remain anonymous, for allowing me to tell their stories.

I appreciate this and God bless you.

Contents

CONTENTS

Introduction

THE WOUNDED STRONG WOMEN

I know many strong women. I have interviewed quite a number of them on my TV Programme, The Standpoint, in its 15 years of existence. Many of them have shared their experiences on the programme; others have done so privately.

On my journey to dealing with my own 'cries', I personally had conversations with some strong women I know, admire, respect and look up to; and they also shared with me what makes them cry!!

Their stories shocked me. Some very nearly left me traumatized. Come with me...

1

THE NO-NONSENSE STRONG WOMAN

Let's call her Madam Tee. She is a no-nonsense advocate and 'implementer' when it comes to child abuse in any way, shape or form. She would give her all to make sure perpetrators received due punishment.

She was "the go-to person" for many people, especially the 'voiceless' and underprivileged. I had worked with her on many cases. No place was too far for her. Besides, she took every case very personal.

But I noticed that she had slowed down in recent times.

So we had a chat.

Madam Tee: "OGA (as most people affectionately call me now), you have no idea what I have been through. My dear, can you believe that as I was out there rescuing and fighting for other people's children, my own child, my only child was being 'destroyed?'

My heart skipped a beat.

Me: How? What happened?

The story unfolded about how her 9-year-old daughter fell ill while she was attending a conference outside the country. She asked her trusted house help to take her to the hospital. Two days later, the doctor sent her a message, asking her to see him on her return.

In the meantime, he advised that her daughter be moved to live with a trusted family member till her return. She told me she panicked and tried to force the doctor to tell her what was wrong with her daughter. But the doctor, a family friend, only said "It's nothing to worry about."

"Gifty, I collapsed when the doctor told me what had been going on. And my daughter, with whom I thought I had a good "buddy-buddy" relationship, confirmed it in the Doctor's presence."

She said, "Gifty, apparently my house help, the girl who had become a daughter to me, and whom I had come to trust with the care of my young daughter, had been sexually abusing her for almost 4 years, under my very nose".

"Jesus!!!" I exclaimed.

"Yes Gifty! With all that I do for others, my own daughter was being sexually abused by my house help, and I did not know it. I didn't even suspect it and my poor daughter had been too frightened to tell me," she added.

The poor child had consequently developed an infection that could negatively impact on her ability to have children in future.

Not only did the house help use her fingers to molest her, she used other objects as well. It's best to stop here and not go into the details of this story, but to tell you the truth, Madam Tee felt she had failed as a mother; and to date, hasn't been able to forgive herself. The situation led to serious marital issues with her husband and they are currently separated. Her relationship with her daughter is also strained. She feels ashamed to let anyone know about it.

For a long time, she felt God had failed her because she was a woman of prayer, and saw her advocacy work as her God-ordained-ministry. So why didn't God protect her daughter? Why? Out of anger and bitterness, she quit church and took a break from all church-related activities

Her confidence was broken, but she kept to herself.

Of course the house help has been prosecuted and jailed, but it doesn't take away the damage, the pain, regret and depression.

She lives in constant fear of the possibility of her daughter growing up and not being able to have children. There is a constant "what if" battle going on within her. This is trauma you can't even wish on your worst enemy.

And please don't ask "Why didn't the girl tell her mother?" Don't get into victim blaming; neither should we ask "How come the mother didn't notice?" Please, don't. No!! Don't!!!

She cries, but hasn't given up. She is spurred on to fight for young girls, particularly, because of her daughter's experience.

2

THE SPIRITUALLY STRONG WOMAN

Lady Cathy is one person who likes to say it as it is. She is very beautiful, loved by many and equally envied. She speaks well and always looks good. She is knowledgeable and commands respect. She has mounted many platforms across the globe. Her husband is openly affectionate towards her. He simply adores her and shows her off like a 'trophy'. (Perhaps that should have been a red light but I guess we, their admirers and cheerleaders, were blinded.)

So what makes "Mama"—this spiritually strong woman—cry every night?

"Gifty, I am even shy to tell you." Just then, she broke down in tears.

I was confused and didn't know what to do.

"It's OK, Mama. It's OK if you can't talk about it. I only came to share my stress with you Mama"

But she opened up, because she had been 'dying' to open up to someone.

"Gifty, my husband is a sexual beast. Not only is he a sex addict, he has strange sexual desires. I have to dress a certain way for him during sex and he only likes to have me through the anus; he does not want it any other way. He chokes me when he is about to climax. Sometimes, he bites me. Many times, I thought I was going to die."

I regretted the question. I mean I regretted asking her about what makes her cry. I wondered if she would be able to look me in the face afterwards. How would she feel knowing that I now know her darkest secret? But support without judgement is what she needs; it is what we all need.

I so much wanted to ask her why she allows him to use her that way, but it wouldn't have been fair to her.

I listened as she continued her story, trying to smile through her pain. "Gifty, I am not staying because of the money, fame or the trappings of being married to him. Gifty, I love my husband. It is strange, but I love him and pray for him. There is nothing God cannot do. He has become so obsessed and possessive of me he accompanies me everywhere and doesn't give me breathing space".

Well, that's enough. I think I am sharing too much. It sounds like something out of a movie, but this is a strong woman's real life story. Who am I to judge her?

A few weeks before writing this book, I had a call from her. "Gifty, I have left him and relocated outside the country," she said.

Incredible! A strong woman definitely has her day! Thank God for her life.

This story may be an extreme case, but we know and have heard of the stories of some Pastors wives who have had to endure a lot in silence. They cry in their closets but have to show up strong in church and elsewhere. Their cases may not be that of sexual bestiality. But neglect, lack of intimacy, no respect, keeping quiet over adultery and idolatry, abuse in all forms and shapes including physical abuse.

3

THE PASTOR'S WIFE

I kid you not. To be a pastor's wife is not easy, especially, in our part of the world. Their cries vary, not necessarily because of their husbands' actions but they face disrespect from church members and other junior pastors. Pressures of the office they hold as pastors' wives also account for some distress, frustrations and sometimes depression.

These women are expected to be "Superwomen". They are burdened with the success of their husbands' ministries, growth of church and so much more. They are supposed to be the prayer machines that miraculously turn things around for their husbands, church, family, etc. They are strong women! It is tough and…yes, they do cry!!

I recently heard a talk about how she started the ministry with her husband, struggling to build on their church membership, going for days without food and pretending to fast. Not being able to attend antenatal or even afford folic acid as a pregnant woman.

She spoke about the days and nights when she cried out to God, wondering when "it would be well" with them. I wonder how many women of today can endure that.

Today, she and her husband, pastor of one of the biggest churches in Ghana with branches all over the world.

But even till today, she still cries…sometimes for joy and sometimes as a result of hurts, disappointment and betrayal.

Imagine being a pastor's wife without a child. Your husband prays for others and they get pregnant. You have been married to him for years, yet you are not receiving your own miracle, your bundle of joy. Imagine!

But Mother Eve cried because her sons, Cain and Abel, became enemies, and Cain killed Abel.

Sarah, Hannah and the Shunammite woman cried because they needed children. Naomi cried because she lost her husband and two sons. Ruth cried because she lost her husband. Abigail cried because her husband was wicked. Jochebed cried because she didn't know the fate of her son Moses as she put him in a basket and watched him float away.

Esther cried because her people were in danger of being destroyed.

Elizabeth cried, too. It took a long time for God to open her womb to conceive. Mary and Martha cried because their brother died and Jesus delayed in coming. Mary Magdalene cried because she was to be stoned.

Mary Mother of Jesus cried because King Herold sought to kill her Son; she cried because she witnessed her son crucified and die a painful death on the cross.

But in all cases, God proved Himself faithful. He always showed up to wash away the tears of those who relied on Him.

4

THE STRONG WOMAN
WITHOUT A CHILD

Lady Rakia (I call her Magagiya) is powerful and rich in her own right. She has it all. She travels the world first class and stays in the best of hotels.

She is an astute business woman and her hands are blessed. Every business she touches becomes successful. And oh, she is a giver. So kind to all who need her help and support.

Raki had a tough upbringing. She was a brilliant girl from a Zongo community. Many people looked down on her because of her background. She came from a big family of 32 children. Her father officially married 4 wives but had children out of marriage.

She became a strong tough woman because that was all she knew to become. She actually had no choice than to be strong. She started fending herself from age 10, doing everything and anything to survive. By the time she turned 21, she had her own shop at Makola (a popular market in Accra, Ghana) selling cloths. Magagiya was business and business was Magagiya.

She was a self-made independent woman before she got married. As such, she feared no one and was nobody's 'walk over' woman. She commands respect wherever she goes. And oh, she knows how to show up big time everywhere. I just love her.

So Lady Raki (yes I have many names for her) lives "large and loud". She is one who is not bothered by anything. She is married, yes, but perhaps her greatest burden is that of childlessness. Her husband, however, has children outside their marriage.

She said to me, "Gifty, I cry every time I have my monthly cycle. I have tried it all, fertility treatment, IVF, etc., but none have worked for me. I even tried surrogacy, but the girl took the babies away and threatened to expose the hospital if they tried to force her to give the child to me."

She added that she had so much hope when I had my daughter but still nothing is working for her. "I know my husband loves me and so to make up for my pain, he treats me like a queen and spoils me as you know. He has refused to marry any of the women he has had children with, but nothing can fill the void created deep within me by my childlessness. I would give away all my wealth just to have a child. But till then, my dear, I will cry while I will live. I will do what I can in the meantime to leave a name and legacy," she concluded.

That was a lot to swallow and yes, we both couldn't hold back our tears.

That's what I am talking about. Making the best of the cards life deals you in the midst of your tears.

And oh, Raki takes care of all 7 children her husband has with 3 different women.

I really don't know what to make of this one, but my respect for her shot up 3 notches.

5

THE STRONG WOMAN SINGLE PARENT

I am not a fan of the title "single mother". Why single mother? Did you make the child or children on your own? Yes, I get it that the man is not in your life or in the life of the child or children, but… anyway, being a single parent can be tough, yet it doesn't mean you are cursed or you are a 'pitiful' human being. It means you need to go the extra mile to play the role of a father and mother in the life of your children. And trust me, there are supposedly married women who do same. The fathers are mostly absent from home and do not provide for their upkeep.

But being on your own without their father supporting can be very traumatizing.

A lady shared with me the heart-breaking story of her son nearly committing suicide because his friends always laughed at him for not having a father.

Another woman told me how her daughter would cry day and night asking to be taken to her father. Meanwhile, she had no knowledge of the whereabouts of the man. Besides, his family don't want to see her. Her daughter blames her for refusing to take her to her father and has started giving her attitude and being rude to her.

She cries because, in her view, she is doing her best as a mother for her daughter, but she doesn't appreciate it.

As tradition demands, when a girl is getting married, her father has to be present. It doesn't matter to her if her father is a dead beat father. Once he is alive, they have to find him to consent to and be present at the marriage ceremony.

I think this tradition must be modified at the very least. I know views like these get me into trouble with some traditional authorities, but to me, it really needs to be reviewed. It causes the mothers so much pain after all that they go through for their children.

The worst is when, after neglecting the children, they later come back to fight for custody and because most of the time, they have more money than the mothers, they frustrate them.

Now, the stories of mothers raising and taking care of children with special needs are just heartbreaking.

These mothers cry a river almost every day. It is completely unimaginable what they go through to find solutions for their children's conditions.

The pains and dashed hopes of going through 9 months of pregnancy with doctors constantly telling you your baby is doing OK, only for you to deliver and after 6 to 12 months and sometimes 2 years, have your child diagnosed with a condition that can only be managed but not treated.

The shattered dreams, coupled with the stigma society attaches to it and the name calling. The fear and 'embarrassment' you feel anytime you have to go out with your child. The insensitive questions asked by strangers. Family members shunning your company as if your child's condition is contagious.

And after all this trauma and lost hope and fears, the father of the child abandons you and blames you for being the cause of the child's condition.

In my view, every mother solely taking care of her child or children is a strong woman and I do understand their tears.

They often deprive themselves of every good thing they desire, for the sake of their children.

Cheers to all mothers, married or unmarried, singlehandedly taking care of their child or children. But to the mothers with special needs children, I say you are the real superheroes!

May your tears never go to waste.

6

THE STRONG WOMAN WHO LOST HER DAUGHTER

"TO NICOLE, THE GIRL WHO WENT ON A DATE WITH CANCER"

I don't remember exactly how I met Mrs. Gloria Abla Pwamang, but she became my makeup artist for The Standpoint TV show for years. Her brand, Makeup and More, became synonymous with the show.

Gloria is a dedicated and loyal entrepreneur. We eventually became like family, so she used to come to the recordings with her children, especially Nicole, who was literally "mummy's handbag". I was therefore, shocked to learn from Gloria that Nicole had been diagnosed with cancer.

Nicole Wesoamo Pwamang (may her beloved soul rest in perfect peace) remains the youngest person to have ever been on The Standpoint as a panelist. "One on One with Nicole: The Girl who went on a date with Cancer and returned stronger".

She was beautiful, intelligent, lively, and active.

At age 11, Nicole was diagnosed with Osteosarcoma, which is cancer in the femur (thigh bone). She was diagnosed in Ghana, but could not be treated in Ghana due to the nature of the condition. She went through chemotherapy, radiation, surgery and post-surgery chemotherapy and physiotherapy in India. She was in India for over 18 months but was cleared on grounds that there was no more evidence of the cancer.

She launched her foundation to support children battling with cancer on my TV Show, The Standpoint, upon her return from India. Her first major project was to raise money to buy a pet scan for Ghana, which did not materialize. She also wrote a book on her experience but did not live to see the launch of the book. At age 14, the cancer retuned and this time, she couldn't survive it. Nicole's book was thus launched post humorously.

It is difficult for a mother to lose a child. But I can only imagine the trauma a mother goes through, knowing that her daughter is dying because there is no cure for her condition and actually watching her die in her presence.

She often tells me she is better now, but Gloria hasn't recovered and I don't think she can ever fully recover. I pray that the Lord continues to comfort her and strengthen her.

The good thing is Gloria has channeled her loss into a good cause, supporting and raising funds for children with cancer whose parents can't afford treatment.

Losing a child is no doubt painful, no matter how old the pregnancy is, or how old the baby or child is. It is painful and I can only imagine a mother's pain.

"I don't know how to tell you this, mummy, but I lost my pregnancy. Mama, I lost my baby. I have cried my eyes out and there are no more tears coming out. I am now moaning, Mama. I am moaning. I prayed, Mama. I prayed so hard but I still lost the baby".

What do you say to a young woman who tells you this over the phone? How do you console such a person?

I was confused when I heard those words from Yaayaa over the phone. First of all, I didn't know she was pregnant. I hadn't heard from her for a while but I assumed she was busy as usual. She is one very determined young woman and very business minded.

Yaayaa is one of the kindest women I know.

She ticks all the boxes of being a good human being.

She already has 2 girls who are "daddy's girls". They are in their teens and she's been praying and trying to have a third child for years.

I actually thought she had given up, until I had that call.

Yaayaa said she was over the moon when she tested positive for the pregnancy. "Finally," she thought. And when, at 4 months old, she was told it was a boy, she was extremely happy.

She said she put everyone on hold and slowed down on all activities. Her complications started when she was 3 months pregnant, but she was trusting God. But I guess God always knows best.

7

THE STRONG WOMAN ON THE BATTLE FIELD OF WORK

Everyone knows Abby is good at her work. No doubt about that. You can say anything and everything about her but her work ethic is impeccable!! A real definition of a fine professional.

But Abby is constantly crying. Nothing she does seems to please her bosses. They always find something to intimidate or demean her with. It's almost as if they have ganged up against her. But she is determined not to let them break her. She goes to the washroom to cry her heart out, polishes up and shows up strong.

Her colleagues call her names because she will not allow the men to sexually harass or pass sexist comments about her.

Her female colleagues, especially the married ones, throw barbed comments at her because she is not married. They tell her, "Even Gifty Anti, after all her "too known", got married when she realised she was getting expired." I didn't know 45 to be equivalent to expiry.

Abby has had it tough, and it didn't get any easier when man after man kept "messing her up." But her decision now is to wait on God's own perfect will. (My kind of girl).

Abby owns a house we call a mansion. She has her own car and a side business. Her work takes her around the world. Abby has changed jobs, God knows how many times. And each time, she lands a 'better job'. She is that blessed, but even with her work at multinational companies, she has had it tough. Frustrations and intimidation in all forms. That girl has suffered. At a point, she felt she was cursed and so started moving from one pastor to another. At one time, she became so depressed she had to be treated at a psychiatric hospital outside Ghana.

Even though depression is a serious mental condition it can be treated. Every mental condition can either be treated or managed when detected or diagnosed early. Like Abby, we are all at risk, and should endeavour to seek early treatment.

Abby is not stopping at adding value to herself, advancing her career, or doing what she loves best, i.e., living and loving herself. But... she does cry.

Abby is not the only single lady who cries because of how society treats her, despite the fact that 'she brings something to the table, has a seat at the table and sometimes is the table.'

Generally speaking, our Society devalues any woman who, in their view, is old enough to marry, but is not married. No one is secure, irrespective of position or 'standing' in society.

I know of female pastors who, because they are single, are not allowed to officiate weddings, counsel couples or preach on certain occasions. There is no end to the embarrassment they go through in public with demeaning, derogatory or sexist comments from the senior and married pastors within the Church!

Female pastors in general, sometimes, have it really tough; they cry but it does not stop them from laboring in the Lord's vineyard.

8

THE STRONG WOMAN
ON SOCIAL MEDIA

Social media is a planet on its own, and yes, women are actively involved on there. But somehow, I don't know if it is the desire of some people to rid social media of strong women—women who are vocal, assertive and champion a cause. Feminists on social media have, it would seem, their own specially assigned demons to attack them.

I am sure the inventors of social media had good intentions. They intended it to be a platform for networking, championing positive causes, doing business, etc. But some people have found a way to turn it into a platform for wickedness.

I have seen and experienced wickedness on social media, but imagine waking up the morning after your special day to find that you are being trolled, insulted, ridiculed and body shamed because of one picture someone posted of you on your special day! Imagine that!

No matter how strong you are, this will break you. It will make you cry and turn your period of joy, excitement and celebration into pain, hurt and sorrow. You will be traumatized and it will take lot to gain your confidence back.

Women have been humiliated for being either plus size or slim.

And yes, as a feminist myself, it breaks me more when I see my gender involved in such despicable acts.

Many women have shared horrible experiences of trolling on social media. Some of them were so pushed to the edge, they became suicidal.

My group of 10 ladies who I had the detox session with have had their own share of social media bullying. They've been called all sort of names because of their activism on social media. They have received threats, their families have been threatened and some of their children haven't been spared.

It's as if, sometimes, people wake up with the desire to make others weep or feel miserable on social media. I need not write too much about how social media has made many a strong women cry because if you can read this book, then I am sure you have a fair idea what is happening on social media. The sad part is that it is getting worse and gradually becoming a 'weapon of mass destruction' for wicked people, most of them faceless. I wonder why some people don't get it that it is not their right to comment on posts they don't like or posts of people they don't like. Yes, it is a choice to either comment or not comment but not a right!

9

NANA AFRAKOMA II, PARAMOUNT QUEEN MOTHER OF AKWAMU TRADITIONAL AREA

The Akwamus have a rich history of being fighters and good ones as that. In fact, the Akwamu stool and the Dormaa stool are twin brothers. History has it that there was a tussle between the twins concerning who should occupy the throne as a chief. To prevent the brothers from 'killing' each other, their mother decided to leave Akwamu with the younger son, some warriors and some of the people, to seek, conquer and rule a new territory.

It definitely takes a strong woman to take such a difficult decision. Leaving one son behind while she steps into the unknown with her other son. I am sure she did cry many times.

Nana Afrakoma was crowned Paramount Queen Mother just when she turned 18. Young, confused and not ready for such a huge responsibility, she cried.

Nana Afrakoma II recounts how she cried many times because she was missing out on the fun that young ladies her age were having.

History also has it that there was a lot confusion, conflict and antagonism surrounding the selection or choosing of a new king for the Akwamus when, her uncle, Odeneho Kwafo Akoto II died. She therefore, had to step in to hold the fort. She held the Akwamu Traditional Area together for over two decades.

She tells her own story…

I would want to briefly discuss what we mean by a strong woman or one who exemplifies a real woman of substance. In 1964, Nana Afrakoma, that is myself, was made a queen mother. I can vouch for the fact that men are quite important in many aspects of our society. However, in earlier eras, before the white man introduced "women empowerment", women had their own power. Why do I say this? Because it was and still is the duty of the woman to choose who is most suitable to be enthroned as a King or Chief.

Indeed, Women are known to be quite powerful in this country and the rest of the world. This emphasizes the Akan proverb "It is always preferable to be counselled by the old woman (Abrewa) in times of conflict or while seeking knowledge.

This best describes an old woman as both knowledgeable and gifted.

This is instructing us as women to take our duties seriously and to fulfill our obligations. We need to maintain the strength that God has assigned to us as women in order to succeed.

Furthermore, the proper functioning of chieftaincy in our society is entirely dependent on the woman. The throne and everything concerning it, are said to have belonged to the woman, but when she gave birth to a son, she decided to give up her place and allow him to rule instead.

As a result, Kings and Chiefs now refer to all women as "Maame," or mothers.

I would encourage all women to remember that because of our strength and can-do attitude, there is no tolerance for laziness or disregard for our obligations. Let's continue to put in the effort as women so that what we accomplish can be recognized and seen.

Instead of tearing down other women, let's endeavor to support and have each other's back. By doing this, we will increase the value of the power that the All-Powerful God has granted us. And let's not forget that nothing accomplished on this planet is ever fully realized without the participation of women.

Being a paramount Queen Mother is not easy. But I, Nana Afrakoma, will say that I also make an effort by inspiring myself every day. You have no idea what I went through—the difficulties I went through before, during, and after the burial of Odeneho Kwafo Akoto II, the former Chief of Akwamu, who was my own uncle.

Ghanaians may recall the unfounded rumors that surrounded the Akwamu chieftaincy. When we needed to choose the right successor, it led to arguments everywhere, and the men firmly said that they would never let me make the choice or dictate to them. Instead of allowing this to discourage or demotivate me, I spoke up for Akwamu and helped them understand my responsibility in selecting the next chief.

While the seat at Akwamu was vacant, it took me more than 35 years to overcome this misunderstanding by fighting my way out with these men and succeeding in the process, thanks to God's grace.

For all these years and to this day, I am still Akwamu's Queen Mother.

I'm begging women not to give up because I know how painful it can be to stay in unhappy relationships caused by careless men. Instead, keep praying and fighting bravely, and the All-Powerful

God will assist you. It is obvious that we cannot eliminate the issues and obligations that God, in His own perfect wisdom, designated for us as women.

I have had my days and moments of crying and I still cry sometimes. But that does not make me any less the strong Queen I am.

As women, let's be strong and prove to the world that we are capable.

10

THE STRONG WOMAN
LEADER

Angela Dwamena Aboagye, née Dua-Sakyi, is an institution! Long before the likes of Gifty Anti, there was Angela Dwamena Aboagye (who now has a PhD in Theology and is a Minister of the Gospel).

She was and still is a household name, well-respected and an authority when it comes to women empowerment. She has trained and groomed many young women who fight for the 'holistic liberation and empowerment of women'. I am one of them.

Her NGO, The Ark Foundation, was the go-to organization if you needed information, education, data, etc., when it came to the 'gender agenda' movement in Ghana. They also had the only well-established shelter for abused women and girls in Ghana, and for almost 25 years, the shelter has been in operation. I have had the opportunity to send some women and girls there myself.

She and others have led many demonstrations, especially in the late 90s and early 2000s when women were being serially murdered in this country, Ghana. She was a loud voice and no one could silence her. No one. She was fearless and we all wanted to be like her.

Dr. Angela Dwamena Aboagye has suffered her share of public abuse because of what she stands for and fights for. The insults, threats, accusations, name calling—she has borne it too. Even her husband and children have had to deal with being asked why she's so adamant about speaking up for women; and whether she's actually a good wife to her husband.

But Angela was our pride. She was our strength, our go-to person and our claim to fame. When we were told that we could not get married because of our stance on women empowerment, we pointed to Angela. For me in particular, she was and still is my "World Cup" partly because I look a bit like her.

However, Angela was going through her own crying moments and most of us had no clue.

She suddenly slowed down sometime in the latter part of 2000, and many of us were wondering what was going on. But thankfully, most of the people she had trained stepped in and so her seeming absence wasn't felt much.

After a few years when I finally reconnected with her, she told me about a book she had written, a compilation of poems and daily devotionals. In this book, published by Xulon, USA (2011) Angela writes some of her experiences in dealing with mental distress over a period of time. Having gone through severe depression and OCD, the book heralds how God had held her through her illness until she had come out of it.

Depression? OCD? The Angela Dwamena Aboagye? How? What happened?

She tells us a bit about what happened.

"Everything was normal, going on well as usual with church, work and family life. But sometime in 2008, I began to experience horrible uncontrollable thoughts and images in my mind, which nothing I knew how to do, could shake off. They were so bad that they began to wear me down even from the mere effort of trying to control them. I couldn't speak to anyone about it because I didn't understand what was going on and had never heard of anything like that. It produced a great deal of anxiety reactions that led me into a deep, dark depression.

It was a "walking through the valley of the shadow of death" experience; something I wouldn't wish even for my worst enemy. When I finally broke the silence to my family and my Pastor, I was really,

really ill. Worse still, I was later misdiagnosed at a facility someone had suggested I go to for treatment, and given all the wrong medications. But praise God that He had my back! He has never been known as a Shepherd who abandons His sheep in times of trouble.

The Lord opened up the nature of my illness through research, (which I did myself), conferences, books, a strong friendship, support of family and PRAYER. God was so gracious that even though I was not fully recovered, I undertook and obtained a Master of Theology and went on to do a PhD, with my thesis focusing on Women's Mental Health and Pastoral Response in Ghana.

Now I share my knowledge with churches, theological institutions, the medical school, and with psychologists and psychiatrists! A lawyer turned expert in identification, diagnoses and treatment of obsessive compulsive disorder (OCD) and related mental illnesses! Only God can turn ashes into beauty; mourning into dancing; and He does not waste a tear! I'm back fully helping survivors of domestic violence and sexual assault victims, by the grace of God. I am also serving in my church family and enjoying the love of Jesus and fellowship with other believers. I'm also grandma to two great boys so far, and praying for more to come as God wills!

Am I a little quieter? Maybe a bit more reflective, more toned down with growth and maturity, but no less passionate about women empowerment, advocating any place there is an opportunity! I still believe that women are created by God as full armour bearers, as men are. I still believe that they hold up half the sky and must have access to all opportunities available to men to do well and contribute their quota to society.

I believe that men and women, particularly those who mean to please God, must emulate Christ in their marital relationships and demonstrate this in their affection and regard for one another.

Finally, I believe that even if we don't get to see equity and justice between women and men achieved in this life, one day, our dear God and Lord of all will make it all right, with no politics or 'isms' attached! Lol!"

11

THE STRONG
YOUNG WOMAN

Positive Energy or feedback is very important when it comes to speaking to an audience. The way they respond can help or disturb your delivery.

I met Maame Esi in 2022 when I went to speak at a church on the Spintex road.

Although she walked in a bit late, Maame Esi is not the kind to miss. She was well-dressed, makeup on point, hair well done and her spectacles were unique.

The people in the room were not many but Maame Esi seemed to be all that I needed to give a good speech that touches the core of my audience. Her responses, shouts, accolades were simply energising.

After the programme, she walked up to me and told me she had been looking forward to meeting me for years. She said she came especially because she wanted to meet me and ask me to mentor her.

"Mummy, I have been through a lot in life" were her first words when we met again at my office.

She is a beautiful hard working young lady and a committed Christian. She is dedicated to the things of God and makes no compromises when it comes to the things of God. She is humble and understands the essence of service.

But she is single and it bothers her. Rightly so because of the 'system' she finds herself. Can you imagine a young woman, speaking at events, encouraging women and yet not married, in our Ghanaian system? The country that condemns every woman who is not married and yet does not care about the success of marriage and child care.

Maame Esi once was in a relationship that everyone thought was going to end in marriage. Everyone had been told about her impending marriage to this man. Her parents knew and had met him and she had met his family too.

Knowing my daughter, she had selected the finest of the fine things, and preparing for the D-day. Then suddenly, the man said he was backing out. Why? He was not comfortable with her; he suspected she would outshine him if they got married. She 'is too much' for him, he claimed.

She became so broken and cried. She reached out to respectable people in society they were both acquainted it to talk to him, but he did not budge. He didn't want the relationship anymore and that was it.

She has not fully recovered from this pain, but she is still soldiering on for God and country.

Thank God for her faith in God. Thank God for her selfless service to God, her tears are watering her strength and she is emerging stronger and better than ever. She has and is becoming a more refined young woman and when that God-ordained man comes, he would definitely find a pure diamond in her.

12

THE STRONG WOMAN IN POLITICS

One of my main reasons for producing The Standpoint was to showcase strong women. Women who, in my view, are intelligent, assertive, outspoken and fearless.

So the first 2 episodes of the show was on Women in Politics. We interviewed a woman who could have been a possible running mate of the then presidential candidate of the NPP. She was capable in every sense of the word. But marriage was being used against her. All sorts of stories were being told about her and why she was not married. So yes, she was not chosen as the running mate. This was in 2008.

Fast forward to 2020, the National Democratic Congress, NDC also chose a woman as a running mate. Lord, have mercy! What brouhaha this generated. A woman who had served in many capacities as the 'first woman' and now the first woman to serve as a running mate in a major political party in Ghana still came under verbal attack. Even her children were not spared.

On The Standpoint, one of the things I sought to find out about women was why they refused to avail themselves for positions of authority, especially in politics. I remember the infamous statement by a former president of Ghana when asked why his government had only a few female representatives, he responded "But where are the women?" Many of us, gender activists were angry at that time. I later on realized that he was right to a certain extent.

But all of these point to one thing: being a woman in politics is not for the faint hearted. It is really tough and many cry.

I got to know women whose marriages failed because of politics. Their husbands and families could not stand the insults, threats, and sometimes humiliation associated with politics. And in a patriarchal society like ours, a woman cannot be allowed to bring the 'name of the family into disrepute.'

If you are single, it will be used against you and if you are married... it comes with its level of attacks.

This problem does not only pertain to Ghana.

I had a conversation with a deputy minister from an East African country whose marriage collapsed because of politics. She told me how even when they got invitations and her name came before her husband's, he would insist they do not honour the invitation because he had been disrespected. His name should have appeared first because he is the man.

She also cited conditions that prevailed when they attended social gatherings such as church services, parties, PTA Meetings. Her husband insisted they sit at the back because they were only being given protocols as a result of her position. He ensured they declined every privilege or special treatment.

Please, allow me to quote a statement the second gentleman of the United States of America, Mr. Douglas Emhoff made, when he and his wife, Kamala Harris, the first female vice president of America, who also happens to be black, visited Ghana in March 2023.

He was addressing an all-girls basketball clinic in Ghana when he said, "It is so great to be in Ghana. We got here yesterday, it was an incredible welcome. Errr...my wife, the vice president, (I love saying that)..." And he had this big smile on his face. Obviously a man proud of his wife's position and achievement.

But Kamala herself had it tough campaigning to be vice president, even in America. However, her husband stood by her and is still standing by her.

But not many women have it that way.

13

WIDOWED TOO SOON

She was his Chioma and he was her Chuku Emeka. The inseparable two. The fine Military General who fell in love with the renowned actress and entrepreneur!!

How Gen. Martin managed to stay sane and married to the now Honourable Abla Dzifa Gomashie for all those years is a mystery. That sister of mine is 'fire'. I can see her rolling her eyes and laughing as she reads this.

Their marriage was uniquely beautiful. There was no way you could get the General on your side when you were fighting or arguing with his Dzifa. At least, not when Dzifa was present. Behind the scenes, maybe, but not when she was present. Don't even waste your time!

Honorable Dzifa Gomashie sums up their relationship this way: "He wasn't perfect. I am not perfect. We chose to make it work for twenty-nine years."

And then one day…it was all gone.

We will all die one day, but General went too soon.

He was sick for a long time, but we all hoped he would get well, but unfortunately, God knows best.

He was her strength during her campaign period and it was a marvel how Dzifa combined campaigning with taking care of General during his long stay at the hospital and still managed to give the NDC its highest votes in both the parliamentary and presidential elections in 2020.

Brigadier General Martin Ahiaglo died two weeks after Dzifa won her elections and she is the only one who can explain how it felt. The emotions she went through.

I wasn't there for her much during those dark times and she was hurt. But she is not the type to keep grudges forever. So one day in 2021, she called for us to meet up and talk. We sat in her car for almost 4 hours, as she poured out, vented, and cried. I admitted that I could have done better and I believe she forgave me. It was a real detox session.

I remember one of the things she told me that cut deep through my heart. She said, "Sis, as I sat in parliament on the 7th of January, 2021, my first day in parliament as a parliamentarian, I picked up my phone to send Martin a message. I wanted to tell him, 'We did it, Martin'. Then I remembered Martin was no more. Sis, I cried. Oh, I cried"

Her husband, Brigadier General Martin Ahiaglo was the one who encouraged her to go into politics and contest for the biggest constituency in Ghana, Ketu South Constituency, in the Volta Region of Ghana.

But suddenly, she felt all alone. Her tears have still not dried up. But still she soldiers on, like the military daughter and wife she is. Yes, she is a military barracks girl. Her dad is a retired military officer.

Honourable Dzifa Abla Gomashie, MP for Ketu South tells her story:

"There's a deep sense of fulfillment that I am experiencing at this stage in my life. First as an artist and now as a politician.

Sometimes, I think I became an artist by accident and sometimes there's a compelling chance that it is divine and not an accident at all.

At about nine or ten years, I recall that my late mother said to our neighbour that "This child of mine popped out of my womb dancing". That was empowerment right there!

She applauded me anytime I danced. She believed that was what I was born to do, but not my father. He wanted me to be a lawyer. Perhaps, I may well be a lawyer someday.

It was therefore a night of two awards when years later he—not my mother—accompanied me to receive an Art Critics And Reviewers Awards (ACRAG) at the National Theatre.

My father agreeing to accompany me was my first award that night. Everything else I have achieved since then is a bonus.

Meeting the "giants" of the industry--Efua Sutherland, Kwaw Ansah, Mohammed Ben Abdallah, William "akpatse" Addo, Grace Omaboe aka Maame Dokono, Alexandra Akoto Duah, Nana Danso Abiam, Efo Kojo Mawugbe, Lord Bob Cole, etc., at an early age is the divine part of my story.

In my adult life, I have had the opportunity to stand on the shoulders of these "giants" to become the first professional performing artist to become a Deputy Minister among my peers.

I anticipate that many more females, going forward, will strive to become like the ancestors who came before me and the giants of the industry who ensured I became who I am.

It is a fulfillment of what I wished for myself as a young creative and performing artist, a taste of being a star, an author, a published poet, and more. I have used Values For Life a Non-Governmental Organisation to give the young people in the creative sector a platform to experiment with their talents and hobbies and also meet the giants of the various domains in the sector, corporate Ghana, and the political elite.

It is my way of saying thank you to the universe. It is my three sixty degrees payback time. It is my gift to the young poet who will be able to weave the greatest web ever and who will pass on the goodness. Each one, teach one, and soon we will all know.

The desire to attend the University of Ghana was so strong as a young mother, I decided to learn some skills. I learned to act, sell tie and dye fabrics, braid hair and work in theatre productions. I also became a restaurateur as I pursued an MPhil at the Institute of African Studies at the University of Ghana.

All that hustle paid off. I made enough money to see myself through the university as an entrepreneur. Those skills brought me economic growth.

These incidents, coupled with my desire to be that shoulder for the next generation, brought about this present status as the first female in the southern part of the Volta Region to be a Member of

Parliament. Nine constituencies in the Volta Region; Ketu South, Ketu North, Akatsi South, Akatsi North, South Tongu, Central Tongu, North Tongu, Keta, and Anlo.

As the Member of Parliament for Ketu South, I am poised to inspire the next generation with my story.

I am committed to ensuring that these young people have the same opportunity as I did, to improve themselves and break the cycle of poverty in their families, and dare to achieve their dreams.

This is my pledge to the youth of my constituency. I intend to use the opportunity given me by the 84, 664 people who voted for me, to be the Member of Parliament to set in motion, the transformation of individuals who will together bring about the change we want to see in Ketu South."

14

THE STRONG WOMEN IN THE DIASPORA

The stories of our women in the diaspora could push this book to a 1000 pages. There are those who toil and send money home to build or buy homes, only for the family members to misuse the money and lie to them.

One of them told me about her own father who had supervised the construction of her house in Ghana, only for him to change the documents into his name and move in with his new wife. Her husband had contributed to the project so you can imagine what has happened to the marriage.

It is also common to hear stories of ladies in the diaspora whose husbands travel to their home countries ostensibly on holiday, only for the women to find out later that they are men with family back home or have children with other women back at home.

Some men even build houses in their home countries without the knowledge of their wives.

There is the story of a woman who worked abroad, day and night, to support a man who had promised to marry her. She did everything for him including building a house in her home country into which the man moved. He was contesting for local elections and this woman mobilized all resources at her disposal, including borrowing funds to support his election campaign. As you may know, elections are driven by money in most parts of Africa.

Well, he won the elections and then proceeded to abandon the woman. He denied promising her marriage and refused to pay back her money, though he had promised to do so. The lady could not raise the money to pay back the loan and was therefore jailed for 5 years.

She has been released but she is not the same person. She has lost her confidence and respect in society.

Many strong women have ended up with psychiatric conditions because of marriage, the desire or the promise of marriage.

15

TRAUMATISED BY ABUSE

The call came around 4am. I could barely hear what she was saying. "Calm down, Sis. What's going on? What's the problem?" I asked. But she continued crying for about 5 minutes.

Why did I pick up her call around that time? Well, I was awake, somehow. It was one of my restless nights because I was going through my own crying moments.

Finally, she said, "Sis, I did it again. Sis, I did it. I nearly killed him. I nearly killed my husband. When will all this end, Sis? When? I'm tired. I'm fed up. How have I offended God?"

Hmmm. You see, in my early days of The Standpoint TV programme, I did a series on women who had been abused from childhood, with a focus on those abused by close relatives, including their own fathers. Sarah (not her real name) was one of them.

Sarah was abused by her father from age 6 till she was 17 years when she run away from home. Like me, Sarah grew up with only her father. At the time we last spoke, which was a few years ago, she didn't know where her mother was. She had looked for her for years and relatives kept telling her different stories about her mother. But she later got to know that her father 'threw her mother out of their home' when she was about 3 years old.

Her father had sex with her anytime he wanted and she had no one to run to. No one believed her when she told her story. No one could believe that her father, a head teacher and church deacon, a respected man in society, could do that. So she was branded a bad girl. This was in the early 1980s and "these things" were either ascribed to the devil, family witches or the girl being possessed.

No one believed her. Those who believed her also told her that she would grow out of it. She should only pray.

Let me use this opportunity to readdress the issue of trauma, especially from abuse. It is often believed that when a child is defiled, she would grow out of it. No, they never do, if not properly addressed. If she does not get psychological or emotional help, it will stay with her forever and adversely affect her throughout her life. She can become promiscuous because she loses confidence in herself and has no sense of self-worth.

Sarah called because she had stabbed her husband; he had tried to have sex in a 'certain sexual position' with her. The demand reminded her of what her father did to her and she resisted.

This was her fourth marriage. Yes, she had been married four times. She is a pretty, very romantic and hardworking entrepreneur. Her experience of abuse by her father had made her very needy and lacking in self-worth. Her idea of self-worth was in being desired by her man.

She bit her first husband's penis when he tried to force her to give him a 'blow job'. It was something her father forced her to do so she hated it and had told her husband she didn't like it without being able to explain why. So she went 'crazy' when the man forced her to go down on him. She bit his penis and that resulted in him beating her mercilessly. Of course, that marriage ended.

The second marriage also had problems arising from sex and positions she didn't like. The third was the same. And the fourth, a Caucasian, was the more serious one. He wanted to experiment with her which brought back horrid memories of the experience with her father flashing before her eyes and so she stabbed him.

This time, it became a police case and her community got to know what had happened. She was embarrassed, stigmatized, disgraced. Thankfully, she had a good lawyer, who was able to get the case settled out of court. But she was never able to fully recover from the shame and so she relocated.

The last time we spoke, she was receiving professional help.

16

THE ONE DRIVEN
TO THE EDGE

She is well-educated. Beautiful. Affable and outspoken. She is fun and noticeable wherever she finds herself. The life of the party. However, Counselor Favor Brown has a story of many tears.

She married the man of her dreams or so she thought. Everybody loved him but he was an abusive man.

Her now ex-husband was very manipulative and always gas lighted. Not only was he adulterous, he was emotionally, psychologically and financially abusive. But he was an angel outside. To everyone he was the perfect loving husband who couldn't hurt an ant. But he was 'killing' Favour inside.

Favour was pushed to the edge…to the point that she attempted suicide three times. Why would a strong, professional woman earning her own money go to the extreme extent of attempting suicide, not once but three times?

That is the mystery of suicidal tendencies. Never judge anyone who tells you 'I feel like killing myself'. Don't. Just take it seriously and seek help for him or her. It is a cry for help. And don't make 'nonsense' of their pain, because we all bear and handle pain differently.

As women especially, we are told to be strong and endure pain in whichever form or shape it comes. This includes pregnancy, which has led to the death of many women and their babies because they were often afraid to complain about the pain they were going through. What a society we live in! Many also stay in marriages till they are 'killed' or till they die from stress or other conditions. Some also end up at the psychiatric hospitals and centers.

The church does not help matters. Often, they put the burden of survival on women and any woman 'who falls short' is not Godly enough or not praying enough. It is tough.

Until recently, attempted suicide was a crime in Ghana. Survivors of suicide were charged for court and given all sorts of sentences instead of being given psychological help. Can you imagine?

Counselor Favor Brown was therefore, one of the happiest women on earth when the parliament of Ghana on 29th March 2023, decriminalized attempted suicide. What a relief!

On her 3 attempts of suicide, her ex-husband, knowing very well the implications of attempted suicide, actually reported her to the police who arrested her.

But thank God for His timely intervention. The officer-in-charge at the time of her arrest had knowledge about suicide and its ripple effects and so recommended that she see a psychologist.

Years later, Favor has become an anti-suicide campaigner and educator.

When she shared her story on The Standpoint, it was the very first time that she publicly talked about it. She felt The Standpoint was the best platform to not only seek for healing but also empower others in similar situations to seek for help.

Through her foundation, Favor Foundation for Life, FFL, she has saved many lives and empowered many others to look beyond life's challenges by being hopeful of a better future, no matter how tough it gets.

Due to her love for mental health awareness, she pursued a Master's degree in Counseling Psychology at the University of Education, Winneba and is now gazetted by the Ghana Psychology Council, GPC, as a Counseling Psychologist.

She is currently in Canada to pursue further studies in Mental Health to help her better manage her NGO.

She remarried a few years after her appearance on The Standpoint. Favour has been happily married for almost ten years now with five beautiful children.

And I was privileged enough to cut her wedding cake when she remarried, because her husband, Mr Brown first 'spotted' her on The Standpoint.

I woke up to the messages below from her the morning after I told her I was going to write a bit about her story:

> *"You gave me a voice when I had none, life when I thought it was better to die and that has brought me this far. I am forever grateful to you and The Standpoint."*

> *"You are my sister for life, my story will never be complete without you. You are indeed God-sent. Love you more."*

> *My response was "It is all to the Glory of God, my Baby sis. I am proud of you and the woman you are becoming, as well as the impact you are making.*

> *Love you plenty".*

17

A ROMANCE WITH CHRONIC PAIN

Preparing for the surgery and dealing with a second divorce at the same time, all the negative stories about spine surgeries in general and what people would say about my inability to succeed in yet another marriage flooded my head for a vigorous march past unabated.

My mind oscillated between the dens of crippling fear at one point and empowering hope at other times. Drowning in the flood of questions, the hitherto laid-back suicidal thoughts began to gain root in my mind. I couldn't imagine living in the vegetative state as described in some of the materials I had read - if something was to go wrong during the surgery. At this point, my functionality had hit ground zero. I needed assistance with everything, including getting out of bed and the love of my life was also gone. Every day had become a bad day–

bad days that could be fixed with a simple decision. Yet I was stuck, unable to make that crucial decision to move forward. I recognized the vacuum that had been created by the ongoing divorce process. Probably because it would have been easier making this decision with Eli, I had gotten used to making decisions with him. I looked around and there was no one to talk to about my deepest fears. Fears about the second divorce, fear about picking up the pieces while on a sick bed.

Who do I talk to about the suicidal ideations without being judged or being told to suck it in? Who do I call on and be seen and understood as a human instead of being called strong? I looked around many times and felt alone. That feeling of loneliness within a crowd of concerned loved ones and family members was terrifying enough to bring back the suicidal thoughts so strongly.

I recall breaking down in tears one late morning when everyone was out, I was home alone - lost in my gloomy thoughts of suicide. (Mum and my big sister Vivian were attending a funeral in the village, the kids and Mavis were at school and work respectively) The suicidal thoughts spread their tentacles around my overwhelmed mind like a large squid grabbing prey at lightning speed. These suicidal ideations stole sleep from me completely. The imagery of living in a vegetative state should something go wrong during the surgery tortured me. I had seen it in my dreams and brooded over it in daydreams. I dreaded the surgery and the hard work of starting life over after another divorce so much I was cherry-picking between a life with perpetual pain or a quiet death—anything just to avoid this risk of surgery. These rattling thoughts moved from doom to glory and glory to doom endlessly - keeping me awake most nights and exhausted during the day.

My mind would drift to my children from time to time. The prospect of them losing me to suicide and dealing with the aftermath by themselves should have overpowered the suicidal thoughts but the gloom was a stronger emotion. The negative voices were louder and unfortunately sensible to me because they were firmly cast on my guilt. I had condemned myself as a failed mother. "What is the use of a sick mother, an inadequate mother to her children?" I would muse in shameless justification. I was having an emotional meltdown and not acknowledging it to get help.

Let me pause here and ask you, "Are you feeling this way right now as you read this paragraph? Please hold on, don't give in to those thoughts, there is an abundance of love, and help all around you. Please speak to someone.

In the middle of my emotional meltdown, Mrs. Josephine Tetteh, a therapist of the Etherean

Mission, a faith-based organization in Accra came to mind strongly. I had met her at the Etherean Mission's headquarters in Accra when GEM visited Brother Ishmael Tetteh the founder. We had wanted Brother Tetteh whose teachings we considered transformative as a member of the first Board to guide the GEM Management team. Brother Tetteh appointed Mrs. Tetteh to represent him on the GEM Board and that was how I got her contact. I dialed her number absent-mindedly, hoping she wouldn't respond, but she did. The moment I heard her voice repeating "hello, hello, hello" I started wailing, lowering myself from the 3-in-1 sofa I had been lying in, unto the floor of my living room while the tears–with mucus traveled down my face freely.

Sensing my emotions, she stayed on patiently as I wailed instead of saying anything to her. I did not attempt to clean my face, I simply let it all out. After about a minute or so of crying, the emotions settled down a little, letting in her calming voice "Where are you my dear?" she asked. "Home" I replied sensing a motherly concern in her tone as she calmly probed further…. "What happened?" she asked "Nothing happened," I replied. "I am just tired. Tired of fighting. Tired of being strong. I just want to sleep and never wake up. I want to just fade away silently. I am tired." I rattled on tearfully. Mrs. Tetteh stayed on the phone quietly listening to me go on and on about being tired of life. "I am sad, I feel dejected, victimized, and alone in a way I cannot explain". I poured out further. When I was done, she calmly asked "Where do you stay?

Would you mind sharing your location, please?" she requested "I can drive to you where you are, hang in there. I am currently at the Ministries area in Accra." "Please don't come, I am ok", I protested, feigning instant cogency, to prevent her from seeing me in my messy state. I reached out for a tissue roll, cleaned my face, and drained out the mucus from my nose. I didn't want anyone to see me in that state. "I am supposed to be a Strong Woman – Strong women are not supposed to cry. We are to suck it in" I said to myself. I am sure not many had seen me cry, possibly, only two people and my pillows had seen that side of me.

I was either an indestructible rock or a normal person who wears challenges as a belt around her waist) I went on defensively in my buzzy head to justify my protest. I bounced back almost immediately to my self-protective warrior state. I bet the guiding spirits of my dearly departed warrior grandmothers might have sensed the impending family shame and sent defensive vibes to the rescue.

"Don't be upset" she said with composure, having probably seen right through my charade. "I am okay now. You don't need to come. I mean it. Thank you for listening to me", I interrupted coyly before she could finish her sentence. "Okay then, it is okay to feel tired and confused. Surgery is never an easy decision to make. In all of it, know there is love all around you, even if you don't see it now. There is help for you as well. You will be fine. Call me immediately if you feel comfortable talking. Don't hesitate at all okay?" She assured me.

"Yes, I will. Thanks again" She said a prayer and hang up after about 15 or so long minutes.

That night, despite the usual pains, I slept quite well. In my sleep, encouraging promptings would intrude saying "Your body is a temple, God protects his own and delivers them from all their trials." Another encouraging thought would follow saying almost audibly, "God didn't bring you this far to let you down. Remember the details of your life's journey so far?

You will overcome this too". "The surgery will go well. Acting on these promptings I stood in front of my mirror and affirmed words like: "If the surgery is what I need, it will be successful. I will recover and be stronger than ever. My bones would heal. All will end in glory." Looking back on the events of the time, I was in a deep hole of depression for sure. And only Jehovah Overdo could have brought me out and sustained me. I am typing these lines with nostalgic gratitude - recalling some of the unfortunate things people had said to me in those dark days. Some said

I was just lazy, I had been cursed and others said my chronic pain was a spiritual attack. Others suggested I had exposed myself to evil eyes by being too loud and sharing too much of my life on social media. In hindsight, I believe one of the actions that helped me the most, was breaking down that fateful day and CRYING OUT FOR HELP!!

It Is Indeed Okay to Cry.

I realized quickly from my experiences that, the imagery of the strong, silent strong woman is an illusion. Often, we think that holding our breath and suppressing our tears of distress is a measure of strength. In fact, doing so makes you suffer needlessly. Vulnerability, which is being open about our pain is the real measure of courage and strength. Crying is a form of giving voice to our feeling of pain, and it should be normal and healthy. Crying or vocalizing pain gets you timely help. I learned this during the labor for Jayden's birth. Because I fought the urge to cry out loud for long, help was delayed until it was almost too late.

When you watch documentaries on animals, it's clear that they shake, run, crawl, and shriek respectively to release the unpleasant sensations that pain creates within their bodies. We as superior animals can do the same by letting our inner being wail in the face of pain. We have a right to do so without shame. So cry when you feel the urge. Do so freely. When you are done, wipe your face and keep up with life knowing that STRONG WOMEN CRY AND WHEN THEY DO, HEALING AND LIBERATION HAPPENS!!!

Yours truly,

Mummy's Avenger, Juliana Ama Kplorfia

18

THE STRONG WOMEN IN THE QU'RAN

LIFE OF ASIYA

Prophet Mohammed (Peace be Upon Him), the great prophet of Islam is said to have mentioned four women, His wife Khadija, His daughter Fatima, Maryam (Mary) mother of Jesus (May Peace be upon Him) and Asiya, the wife of Pharaoh, as the women that reached perfection.

Other scholars have also identified her as Hazarat Asiya.

Asiya was a queen, the wife of Pharaoh, one of the most powerful men to walk the earth. Though Pharaoh was the most powerful, he is also described as arrogant and a tyrant who ruled Egypt.

However, his wife, Asiya remained a Pious Lady.

Although she feared her husband would agitate against her faith on seeing her pray, she was never demotivated. She worshipped God and prayed always, though in disguise.

Asiya stood firm and walked steadfast in her faith until Pharaoh, her husband who felt she was rebelling against his tyranny tortured and had her killed upon discovering her monotheism.

She was a woman who never allowed herself to be defined or limited by her painful circumstances, but rather carried in her such a deep faith and sense of self that she was willing to die for what she believed in. She refused to submit to the tyranny of her husband. Instead, she chose to devote her soul and life to God.

And it was for this reason that Prophet Muhammad mentioned her as one of the greatest women of all time.

Throughout her life of unparalleled wealth and luxury, she knew that her true home was in Paradise. This juxtaposes her life to be very symbolic, as well as an exemplary of a woman who chose paradise over all the glitters of this world.

Asiya accepted Moses into her home and convinced Pharaoh not to kill him. Her mind and her soul remained independent from her husband since her heart was not enslaved to his beliefs.

There is a lot to draw from the story of Asiya. Her love for God inspired her to take on the greatest W

H E N S T RO N G WO M E N C RY - O G A tyrant of all time and sacrificed her life in the process.

She is said to have always called on God to deliver her from the iniquities of her husband.

Asiya was no ordinary woman. Her strength and status will forever remain unsurpassed. Her character stands out and she continuously leaves an exceptional character for women.

Having sought closeness to her Maker and knowing the life of the hereafter to be better than her luxurious life with Pharaoh, she prayed to God thus,

> *"My Lord, build for me near You a house in Paradise and save me from Pharaoh and his deeds and save me from the unjust people"*
> **—Quran 66:11**

What we learn from her character is that, sometimes we hide behind our comforts and luxuries to avoid doing the right thing. We fear the repercussions of what people will say, what they will think of us, and what will be taken away—a job, an acceptance to school, friends, family—but we never really think about the fact that if we don't act as Asiya did, what's really being taken away is our own beautiful hereafter.

Asiya did indeed live righteously and in submission to the will of God and not man... and that's true faith and perseverance.

But you can imagine the tears—the many times she cried and even the last minute inner cry before she was killed.

19

THE STRONG MOTHER WITH A CHILD WITH AUTISM

Mrs. Mary Amoah and her daughter, Nana Yaa, have become iconic figures in Ghana, Africa—and I dare say the world, when it comes to Autism Awareness.

I remember when Mary, who coincidentally shares a birthdate with me, had to share her story for the first time, on The Standpoint in 2009. Oh Lord! It was tough. Very tough. Without exaggerating, I would say we spent almost 3 hours to record the 45-minute programme. She broke down many times during the show, crying her eyes out. She wanted to opt out but I didn't let her, because I just had a feeling her story was going to make a very great impact.

I later found out that it was the first time she was breaking her story. Her family, church members and friends did not know that her daughter had autism.

I don't know why but I find it uncomfortable referring to anyone as being autistic. It doesn't feel right to me.

She was right about her fear of breaking her silence and letting the world know about Nana Yaa's challenges. The backlash and negative reactions were massive. But she has no regrets, because through that, she is now a world advocate and authority on autism. Her boldness, regardless, has emboldened others too.

Mary has 3 biological children. She had two boys first, so you can imagine her joy when her third child turned out to be a girl. "Finally! I am going to have a little sister and friend. Thank you, Lord". Her joy was out of this world.

However, after 2 years of worrying about Nana Yaa's seeming development delay, she was diagnosed with autism.

It's been a journey of tears for Mary since then.

The fear of rejection and the reality of it all.

The fear of stigmatization and the reality of stigmatization.

The fear of frustration, lost hope, stress, near depression and the realities thereof...

Mary has been through it all.

I expect her to write her own book and tell her

own story.

But Mrs. Mary Amoah has done a fine job raising Nana Yaa. She has given hope to many people raising children with autism by sharing her story openly, though not without tears.

Nana Yaa is now a top model and has also progressed so beautifully. From not being able to say a word to actually holding a conversation even if it's for a minute, singing and sometimes giving her mother attitude just like any teenager.

For any mother raising a child with special needs, every little progress is worth celebrating.

Mary is admirably strong. She never shies away from speaking up about her frustrations and will sometimes cry openly.

Let me take this opportunity to also commend Mrs. Mercy Osei-Ghansah, a young lady after my own heart, for the sacrifices she has made and is making for the sake of her son Raphael who has autism.

Mercy has progressed from denial, to crying and then to acceptance, commitment, advocacy and educational campaigns on autism.

Yes, she still cries but is determined to do her best for her son.

20

WHEN THE FIRST PREGNANCY BROUGHT TEARS

I met Justina Yiadom-Boakye in 2015, about eight ago. She wrote to me just after my wedding and told me she had a story. I gave her my number and we started talking.

Justina has a beautiful daughter called Ayeyi. Ayeyi is her first child and she has a special condition known as OI.

We have been through tough times together. I cried many times without letting her see it because I am supposed to be her mother, the stronger one, the one she runs to and confides in, the one she vents to without fear.

By the grace of God, I have 'held her hand' through some really tough times. I gave her a platform, The Standpoint, to share her story with the world and seek support for her foundation,

Osteogenesis Imperfecta Foundation Ghana. But I always wonder how she does it.

Justina tells her own story better.

"As a newly wedded young lady, I was overjoyed when the doctor confirmed me pregnant just after 3 months of marriage. My whole attention was centered on the bundle of joy that was growing inside me so much that I became so particular about my lifestyle. I wanted to remain very healthy and fit for the child to grow well.

My dream was to hold a healthy bouncing baby in my arms, and cuddle and watch her grow. But at 28 weeks down the pregnancy, this dream became shattered. My whole life took a different turn.

"It's a girl," the scan technician mentioned, and I smiled. "Madam, have you had a fall?" he asked. I lifted my head from his bed and asked why. "There's a problem," he continued, raising an eyebrow. "I can't see the baby well; you need to see a radiologist for a detailed scan," he explained. Suddenly afraid and confused, my heart jumped.

I left saddened. Early the next morning, I was in a radiologist's office for the detailed scan, and lo and behold, he asked me again: "Did you fall?" I replied NO, with much concern. The room went quiet after his question as he continued his work. After all was done, he handed over to me an envelope containing the result. Now, I knew there was a problem. I pulled a very worried face as I sat down in front of my doctor and handed him my result.

Justina, I am sorry to say this, but your baby is not formed properly. The limbs are all deformed. I will advise you terminate the pregnancy. I stared at him in total shock. I knew I had taken all my medications well and stayed very healthy. There and then I started to weep. He advised me to discuss it with my husband and reach a decision with him.

The breaking of this news made me confused. For days, I would cry and pray earnestly to God for a miracle to happen since my husband and I had decided that termination was not an option for us due to our Christian values.

Sometimes, when faced with difficult situations, we tend to compel God to change the situation to our comfort, forgetting that His ways are not our ways, neither His thoughts our thoughts. I carried the pregnancy through to full term, hoping a miracle will happen for my baby but it never happened.

On the 2nd of September 2011, my diagnosed deformed baby was born through a C-Section. The sound of her cry made my heart jump with fear— great fear and, lo and behold, her limbs were all deformed.

That day was the saddest day of my life. My bundle of joy; yet my joy had turned sour.

Days later, the pediatrician broke the news to me and my husband that our baby was suffering from a rare genetic condition known as Osteogenesis Imperfecta. She explained her bones were very brittle and could break easily, and that there was no cure for the condition. Her chance of survival was 50%. I became terrified and started wondering in my mind how to manage a baby with such a condition.

We were handed a paper with the name of the condition on it and told to go read about it.

My first baby in life? Oh God, why me? That was my everyday question to God. After a week at the hospital, as young as I was, I came home with my baby broken all over.

It's been twelve years since.

She survived. Yes, she did. Through hard work, she has made it through.

There was no knowledge to her care. I had to go through with her, with a lot of trial-and-error approaches. There were days she would cough and break a rib. For twelve years, I have learnt to stay strong for her. She has built my inner tenacity and taken all my fears away.

Now my baby has become a rising Star. She has been a voice in Ghana and Africa, advocating for children with her condition. She is contributing immensely to the redefinition of disability in Ghana. Her name is Ayeyi and my journey with her has given hope to many.

Through it all, I still cry with her. I cry and build more strength.

21

A SPECIAL DEDICATION TO THE STRONG WOMAN DETERMINED TO LIVE, REGARDLESS

"This chapter is dedicated to a woman I loved and admired from afar. She became my sister and source of strength when I got closer to her. A woman whose faith is out of this world and who lives life to the fullest each day, though she knows many people with her condition have not survived one hundredth of what she has survived.

She was given a few months to live but has survived for years.

She is Maxine Kyeiwaa Sencherey, affectionately called Kyei Wizzy.

Dearest Sister Mine, I hope you write your book to tell your own story, soon. But thank you for allowing me to tell a bit of your story in this book. I love you sis."

22

THE KYEI WIZZY MIRACLE

Kyeiwaa is an enigma. Love her, hate her, she is Kyei Wizzy. She loves life and has always loved life. To those who don't know her story, she is the party girl. Wherever there is fun, she is there. Full of smiles and laughter. Friendly towards everyone.

To those who know her story… There are 2 groups:

Those who understand her, and support her to live her life to the fullest; and those who feel she must live life cautiously and possibly stay away from the public eye.

She grew up in Accra, Ghana, and Italy. She was a 'tomboy', always with the boys but had a great taste in fashion and always dreamt about pursuing a career in fashion when she grew up. And she fulfilled her dream by working in the fashion industry in USA as a personal shopper for the Hollywood stars.

Kyeiwaa loves pink, a no brainer, because she not only was she born in October but she is also a THREE TIME BREAST CANCER SURVIVOR. Yes, you read right. She has survived Breast Cancer three times.

She says it all started about 20 years ago when she noticed 3 boils under her armpit. She tried everything including herbal treatment but the boils were still there. Later on she felt some pain in her breast and that was when she became alarmed. Her then husband who was in the UK, advised her to come to the UK for medical checkup.

The doctors took a look at it, took some samples for further tests but were so sure it wasn't cancerous because cancer normally doesn't come with pain.

She returned to Ghana a few days later, only to be asked to return to the UK because the sample taken for further tests didn't look too good; they suspected breast cancer. You can imagine her shock and fear.

She returned to the UK. Her husband picked her up from the airport, straight to the doctor's clinic where the doctor confirmed that she had breast cancer.

Narrating her reaction that day to me (in 2021), she said, "Gifty, I cried so much the doctor and nurses also cried. This was 19 years ago, Gifty, and cancer was not openly talked about. Everyone who had cancer had died or was dying. So my reaction stemmed from the thought that I was going to die. I was in my 30s, Gifty. I shouldn't just die like that. My only child then, my son, was just turning 10 years. I cried so much, Gifty."

When she calmed down, she was given the option of having a mastectomy (removal of her breasts) or a lumpectomy (taking out the lumps and nodes, etc). After days of crying and reflecting, she opted for the lumpectomy, though that was a more complicated procedure and would require that she stay longer under anesthesia.

Family and friends advised her to opt for the mastectomy but she said "those were the heydays of Kyei Wizzy, so I wanted to keep my beautiful breasts intact". She has such a great sense of humour. "In any case, I had had about 15 surgeries before then, so I wasn't scared of the surgery", she added.

She did the surgery; lumps and nodes were taken out and even had a booster on the neck. She went through chemotherapy and the whole cancer treatment procedure because the cancer was aggressive, i.e., grade 3. She was then given the all clear medically and told she could live between 5 to 15 years.

Kyeiwaa gives credit to her then husband for being the earthly reason for her survival of the first phase of breast cancer. "He took me to chemotherapy, he took care of me, cooked and made sure I got well."

She also gives credit to the many people who prayed for her when they heard her story, especially, her social media followers.

In the 15th year, after the first surgery, the cancer resurfaced. This time, in the right breast. (The first time was in the left). And this time, she had no choice than to have a mastectomy, in India. The cancer then spread so she had no choice but to have both breasts removed.

Interestingly, the right breast healed beautifully but the left breast, which was affected the first time, refused to heal. It kept her in India for over a year. She said for 11 months, it was not healing and you can imagine the pain, fear and sheer anxiety she went through. "Gifty, I called all my pastors and prophets to pray for me because again, I was not ready to leave this world. My son was old enough. He was now 25, so he could survive on his own. But in the 15 years before the cancer resurfaced, God brought a little girl called Josie into my life and for her sake, I had to be strong and make sure I get well and come back home," she said.

The third time was scary.

In 2020, she went back to India for a checkup and again they saw something and wanted her to stay a bit longer, but Covid had started and so she came back home to Ghana. Not long after that, she fell ill, not from Covid though, but she didn't want to go to the hospital because she was afraid of Covid in view of her underlying issues.

When it got worse, she asked to be taken to the hospital. At the hospital, she started foaming from the mouth and in her words, "I was going." She could see everyone in the room and everything that was going on but no one could hear her.

She was placed in an ambulance and taken to Korle-Bu Teaching Hospital, but there was no bed. Then to Ridge Hospital, still no bed. She kept drifting in and out of consciousness while in the ambulance. She was taken back to Korle-Bu and rushed straight to the emergency room. She stayed at Korle-Bu for about 3 weeks, and after a series of tests, they realized that the cancer had spread to her lungs and spine.

Lord, how much can one person take?

She says it was when she was told about this new development that she realized that perhaps her mother, who was a top baker and great cook in her time, probably died from lung cancer without knowing. She said the autopsy report showed that her mother, who died at the age of 54, had one of her lungs burnt. And there she was at the age of 54, on a hospital bed, being told that the cancer had spread to her lungs.

Her mother died on the date 19th July, and she received the diagnosis of lung cancer, also on the same date, 19th July.

"The devil is a liar," was my impulsive response when she told me this 'unholy' coincidence.

I know she will laugh when she reads this, but Sister Kyei Wizzy is both stubborn and a rebel. She lives life on her own terms, though cautiously. She took some time off to 'breathe' as she put it, before she went to see the doctor with her test results. The doctor was shocked she had survived the three weeks after the diagnosis.

Kyei Wizzy is now at stage 4 with cancer. There is no cure for her. But she continues to laugh and have fun. She enjoys life and takes it one day at a time.

Many people do not understand how she carries on, knowing that her condition is a 'death sentence', yet she doesn't seem bothered. She goes out having fun. She is almost always on Facebook, posting pictures and videos. But Sister Kyeiwaa says Facebook and the outpouring of love from her followers has been a source of strength for her. "Living life to the fullest and keeping a positive attitude while trying to live life as normally as possible is what has kept me so far, Gifty," she concluded.

But she cries… and often. For Christmas 2021, we featured her and her friends on The Standpoint and she cried a river.

23

STRONG WOMEN AND MARRIAGE

I have come to realise that MARRIAGE HAS MADE MANY STRONG WOMEN CRY. Let me state here, categorically, that I am not against marriage. I know there are some really good marriages that have stood the test of time.

But this book focuses on WHAT MAKES STRONG WOMEN CRY.

Just imagine being a CEO or top executive of a company, achieving laurels and receiving accolades everywhere, but when you get home, the one person you hoped would be your top fan or cheerleader, is the one who makes you feel worthless and breaks your confidence. It robs you of your self-worth.

My sweet last baby auntie, Mrs Victoria Quaiyson, who we affectionately call Aunty Vic, calls marriage "beautiful nonsense". I laugh anytime I hear that.

I know and believe that marriage was created by God and all religions of this world believe in marriage. It is supposed to be a beautiful thing but the human beings, the 2 human beings who go into it often find a way to mess it up. How they do it is still being 'analyzed by experts.' Not funny, but sometimes you can't help but laugh.

Too many women have had their 'strength stolen' because of marriage. Every woman, I dare say 99 .9% of women, go into marriage with their all— heart, soul, body, mind. Determined to give of their best. Determined to achieve the 'together forever' status.

But most of the time, a few months, if they are lucky, a few years into the marriage they find themselves wondering and asking themselves "What happened" or "What is happening?"

A woman will be excited about getting married especially when she is over the "acceptable age", to finally be rid of society's stigmatization.

I remember when one of my friends-turned-sisters got married. We were all excited. She actually banned me from attending the main event because it was her day and she "didn't want the focus to be on 'the Gifty Anti' (her words not mine). So I didn't. But at the reception I 'dirtied' myself. What! I danced like David did in the Bible. I was tired of the name calling, so if one of my 'tribe of getting old sisters' was marrying, it was my bragging right.

Not long afterwards, we realized that she had started 'pulling away from some of us.' Especially, those of us who were not married and were vocal in our views about marriage and seemed to be enjoying our singlehood. Some of us suspected what was going on, but then she always had an excuse for not getting in touch anymore.

A few years into her marriage, after not hearing from her for a very long time, she called one night crying and asking me to 'save' her.

Amidst tears, she informed me her husband had been abusing her— physically, psychologically, emotionally. I could not believe my ears. It was so bad, I rushed to the police station that night and got the man arrested. The following day, I had a call from the police station that my friend had come to deny the story and claimed I fabricated it out of jealousy about her marriage. Yes, you can imagine my shock, anger, disappointment and embarrassment.

Her husband and his family even pushed for my arrest and prosecution for falsely accusing their son. But thank God for the wisdom of the police officers who were on duty that night and saw the bruises and blood on my friend, who actually even lost a tooth.

She was a well-established woman—a professional, doing well on her own. She had houses and cars. She was the light of her family. The provider and source of pride. She was well-respected at church and in the society. The only thing she lacked, according to societal standards, was marriage. So she decided to get married, and to a 'sweet guy'. Oh, he ticked all the boxes and so we all were happy for her.

What was the cause of the constant abuse? He was threatened by her financial independence and wanted her to put his name on all her assets.

Well, she stayed married for reasons best known to her and I will not dare judge her.

However, in 2021, after blocking me for over 7 years, she sent a message to ask me to please look for and take care of her children. At the time, she had 4.

As I write this book, my friend has been diagnosed with many conditions. Her husband has married a second wife and treats this new wife like gold.

My friend has literally lost it all and her children.

Her children, oh Lord! I struggle with tears as I write this, her children aged, 14, 13, 11, 9 and 6 (she had a 5th child) have been distributed amongst family members. The poor children have been separated.

My friend was a strong woman in every sense of the word and thankfully, seems to be climbing out of the mire and has started rebuilding her life. It is not easy for her; it can't be. She feels ashamed, guilty and embarrassed, but she keeps going and pushing and I know, very soon, she will be back on her feet.

Her pastor and the church elders kept telling her to pray and that everything would be ok. Yes, I believe in God and I know that what God cannot do does not exist. But the same God has given us wisdom and He expects us to use it and encourage each other in times of difficulty.

I have heard many motivational speakers say that you must 'marry right', In fact, I used to say same too. Some say you must marry a supportive husband.

But the thing is, in this world of pretense and make believe, a world where people have mastered the act of deceit, can a woman really know the true character, nature and motive of a man? And in some cases, the welcoming family?

Many a strong woman has been broken because of the actions and/or inactions of in-laws. But I am a believer in not blaming the mother in-law or sister in-law so much for the simple reason that the man, even if his upbringing saw him pampered, is old enough to learn and unlearn what is right and what is wrong.

Stature and status in society are often used against the woman. Anytime there is a problem, strong women are the target.

They are to blame because they are the strong and vocal women. I remember a woman sharing a comment her mother-in-law made to the effect that she would be the one to be disgraced if issues of her husband's adultery came out.

Her payment for being hardworking and bringing in income rather than stay at home, fold her arms and watch her family starve, was infidelity.

Delayed childbirth or infertility is also another issue that makes strong women cry. Especially those who want to have children of their own.

We have heard real life stories, not in movies. But then again, I have come to realize that most of what we see in movies do happen in real life.

A woman is easily insulted for her seeming inability to bear children. And if you are perceived to be one of the strong women, especially in the public space, then they will make sure you cry every day.

You see, so long as you come across as a strong woman, you will be blamed for everything that goes wrong in a relationship, be it marriage, boyfriend girlfriend, siblings, colleagues. You will be judged and condemned before they hear your story.

One of the women I interviewed on my show, The Standpoint, shared a very sensitive story. (By the way, I am one of those who believe that you must never confront or fight your husband's issue on the side. Never! And I will tell you why, but that does not mean the other woman is free from blame, especially, if she knows the man is married or knows the man's wife. She had a choice to turn him down but she chose to be with him, regardless. So she cannot claim 'innocence' or be 'blameless.')

She belonged to a group of friends. Some married, others not married. They called themselves sisters. They shared their problems; they were together in almost everything. They were admired by many and others wished to be like them. They knew each other's husbands and partners. There was no bad blood; they had each other's back, or so it seemed.

Until one day, one of them—let's call her Adwoa—had an issue with her husband and shared it with her 'sisters'. An issue of—yes—your guess is as good as mine—adultery. As sisters, they were all angry and said a lot. No one was spared, including the man's family.

A few weeks after the incident, the man's family called for a meeting with Adwoa and her family. At the meeting, a tape was played of all that was said at the 'sisters meeting' where the man and his family were 'dissected'.

No, wait! You haven't heard the worst yet. After Adwoa had been harassed and embarrassed, she was informed that since her husband "is a useless man"—something she said at the 'sisters meeting,' he would be marrying someone else; she could leave or stay. Whatever her decision, there would be a second wife.

The said second wife was invited into the meeting and guess who it was? Sister Gee, one of her sisters from the group. Initially, Adwoa thought it was a joke. She collapsed when the reality dawned on her. Sister Gee, her trusted 'sister' had apparently been having an affair with her husband for years.

The group as you can imagine, is no longer together. It is divided into 3.

A strong woman cries when her gender, especially those she thought she could trust, BETRAY her.

Oh, how I wish I could tell you about my recent betrayal by someone I called 'sis'. While I thought I had a safe place to vent, I was apparently being recorded...

24

MY PERSONAL CRIES

My "crying" journey... Yes, I have been called strong by many. Many people have told me how they feed off me and are able to keep going because I give them strength through my write ups, videos, shows, interviews. In fact, some say my whole life gives them strength.

People are quick to tell me "You can handle it, you are strong." If only they could see my deep scars. Thank God some of our ugliest scars do not show on our faces.

No matter how deep and ugly a scar on your face or any part of your body is, it can be fixed with surgery. But how do we fix the scars buried in our hearts and souls?

Where do I start?

I have always carried this 'strong woman' aura right from my childhood days. In primary and secondary school, I was the outspoken girl who was involved in 'everything' including demonstrations and protests, yet I got easily broken and cried a lot.

Professionally... well, let's hold on to that for another book because that experience is a movie with many parts. There were days when I would be crying while presenting the news, but the world only saw a smiling person, well dressed in her slit and kaba, with her scarf nicely tied.

The insults, accusations, rumors, name-calling, gossip, falsehoods that I had no opportunity to defend. Oh, Lord!

So let me focus on the part of my journey that really threw me to the "wolves" of this world.

I have always been that woman on TV that many people looked up to, both young and old. The one that most people wanted to be like. The one often accused of one thing or another. The one who was stigmatized and gossiped about. The one... but when I got married...

How It Began...

25

BEING MARRIED TO A CHIEF NEEDS A DIFFERENT KIND OF 'ANNOINTING'

Let me tell you how I perceived my marriage would be like, before I got married. My husband holding my hand and our child sitting on the his shoulders while we went for walks.

Ok, now let's get serious.

If you've read my book Fifty Nuggets @50, you would know I married late. I was as independent as it could get. I had my own company and hosted my own self-produced TV show for 8 years in my own studio. I owned a car and a house. I was well-established, you could say, by the grace of God.

Getting married to my husband wasn't a difficult decision for many reasons, one of them being that although a traditional ruler, my husband was very liberal and well exposed. We were both in our mid-40s, so we felt we had it all 'covered'. We were old enough and had 'lived' and so were good to go. No pre-marital counseling; we did not need it, we thought. Yes, that was us.

However, it wasn't long before I was hit with the harsh realities of marriage. Well, the kind of marriage in which I found myself, I think I underestimated the 'power and force' of the traditional system. I went in as the woman in the national space fighting and being a voice for women. I didn't understand that the dynamics of being married to a traditional ruler would be very different from other marriages.

Here I was, a well-established independent woman, having to conform to certain traditional 'rules and regulations'. It was tough, but I tried, determined to fit in nicely without causing too much trouble. It was definitely impossible avoiding trouble totally. I tried to do my best, but it was hard. There was only so much I could take. I realized I was losing myself and it was eating me up. "This is not the Gifty Anti I am". I battled with myself and my conscience constantly.

Even my 'language' as a feminist and gender activist was changing. I was becoming a "traditional woman", required to act all "grown up and mature" suddenly. Now, that is not a bad thing but that is not me. I am Gifty Anti, I am unorthodox in my ways. This new me, having to be "traditionally mature and composed" was a bit of a challenge at times and I didn't like it.

Some within the gender movement started to attack and mock me, maybe deservedly so, because I was 'breaking away' from our norm.

At a point, I felt this drastic change was self-inflicted but with the benefit of hindsight, I realize I didn't 'inflict it on myself'. The 'system' demanded it and consciously or unconsciously, I responded.

It was a rollercoaster of emotions. There was talk about me 'betraying the feminist movement' by getting married in the first place. And the almighty accusation of me getting married when all the while I had 'deceived young women into not getting married'. Some went as far as to call for an apology from me. To date, no one has as yet been able to provide the evidence in words or visuals where I supposedly told young women or implied that they should not get married. I have always maintained that marriage is not a must for everybody and no one should be compelled to get married when/ if they are not ready. I maintain my position that marriage is not an achievement; it is not a trophy. But I never forbade anyone from getting married.

At the same time that all these accusations were peddled against me, I was going through a lot of battles, emotionally, psychologically and mentally in my marriage. Yet I tried to keep it all together because 'I am a strong woman' and I constantly projected myself as such.

I vented in many ways but no one understood what was going on. I cried many times but my tears were buried deep inside.

Some within the 'traditional system', sometimes openly and deliberately passed demeaning comments about me in public. And sometimes their actions! Lord, have mercy. Yet I kept quiet, because I didn't want to ruffle any feathers. And I guess I cried most of the time out of my frustration at not be able to react or retort the way I would have loved to, all in the name of trying to conform to the new standard set by my new status.

Nana, my husband, did his best to protect me. He insisted I get the best traditional protocols deserving of a Chief's wife. But that started 'amassing opposition and enemies for him within the 'system' because that was not the 'norm'.

A typical example was once when we attended a programme. I was given a chair next to him at the reception. One of the chiefs noticing this, quickly asked a queen mother to take the seat. She responded that it was meant for me. The chief then remarked, "Wives do not matter when it comes to traditional gatherings". Yes, he said it loudly and he was not joking. There were people in the room, both young and old. I was embarrassed; very embarrassed. But I told the queen mother it was OK for her to take the seat. I then served my husband, making sure he had his drinks and food and quietly exited.

I am blessed to have some 'strong' older queen mothers who back me in many ways but it doesn't make my survival in the system any easier. I try my best to show respect and humility, but there will always be 'those ones' who will find a way to make you 'cry'.

I wonder how other chief's wives are coping though because I know most of them go through similar situations.

Thankfully, I have mastered the act of crying without letting it change me or detract from my purpose and goal.

Interestingly, I have become a reference point for women whose husbands are about to be made chiefs, and young ladies who are about to get married to chiefs. They turn to me for advice and guidance.

God surely has a sense of humour.

26

THE CRY FOR A BABY

I remember in 2011, when my then doctor , broke the news that my tubes were blocked and that it was impossible for me to get pregnant the natural way. My options were artificial insemination or IVF. Oh my God, I cried. I cried like there was no tomorrow. My whole world was shattered.

IVF was not that common in those days. Aside being far too expensive, there were also all sorts of misconceptions surrounding it. It is still expensive though and beyond the reach of many women who want to have children but can't conceive the natural way.

So to me, then, it was the end of the road when it came to childbearing. But thankfully, my boyfriend then could afford it and therefore encouraged me to try it.

It is no secret to anyone who has read my books, follows me on social media or has ever listened to me on any platforms and/or interviews, that Doctors felt it was literally impossible for me to have a child. I made no secret of this before we got married.

One of my favorite topics whenever I have had to speak to young people is "While you wait…" maybe I should write a book on that soon.

I always tell them that it is important to know one's health status and have a frank discussion with one's partner before marriage. You don't have to wait till you are married before you discover your health challenges or otherwise. This is to both genders.

I knew my health challenges, vis a vis childbirth but I desperately desired a child, not because I was married or because of the 'throne'. I wanted a child for ME. I have made no secret of the fact that I had tried IVF thrice in my previous relationship. So yes, I wanted a child for me.

And oh, those 3 previous times I tried IVF, I died every time the results came out negative. The two weeks of waiting to find out the results. The fears, mixed feelings, anger. What if it doesn't work? What if it works? Was I really ready to face the W H E N S T RO N G WO M E N C RY - O G A public ridicule and name-calling of being pregnant and having a child out of wedlock? Was I going to be able to proudly tell the world who the child's father was? Was I really sure that I didn't care about the possible backlash?

Oh, I cried!

But with the benefit of hindsight, I think societal pressures also contributed to pushing me to consider IVF, though I was not married.

So you can imagine my joy when I got married in 2015 and my doctor told me on 29th March 2016, that my womb was fine and I should be able to carry a baby! I was excited but still apprehensive because of my previous experiences. However, I still went ahead with the treatment.

Fertility treatment by itself can be a traumatic experience. The injections, medications and cost involved on the one side and the 'what if' thoughts that flood your mind and threaten your sanity on the other. The fear of it not working. The harrowing two weeks of waiting for feedback that feel like 200 years of agony. The journey of waiting to know whether or not the results would be positive. Oh, I cried buckets.

Well, guess what? The first attempt after I got married, didn't work. But I had a God sent Doctor who was determined not to let me give up. He literally forced me to try again in December that same year, 2016 and this time my miracle and testimony manifested. As I like to say, "It ended in praise". But it was a traumatic journey filled with tears and fears. And even with the final confirmation of pregnancy on 24th December 2016, came yet another journey of fear.

I didn't have an easy pregnancy. I was a 47year old, mother-to-be. I was even afraid to use the washroom for fear of the baby coming out.

27

THE PREGNANCY TEARS

Pregnancy for every woman, especially, a married woman who desperately wants a child, should be met with joy and excitement. However, my joy and excitement were short lived; fear took over.

I will elaborate much more on this journey in my next book, The Black Chale Wote: The Story of the Late Bloomer. But let me share a little bit about the tears on this journey.

It was a lonely journey for me. Very lonely. Filled with many tears and hurts. I kept the pregnancy private, though a part of me desperately wanted the world to know I was pregnant. I wanted to share my joy with the world. BUT I was afraid. What if…? What if I lose the pregnancy? What if I lose the baby? What if…?

Being in my profession, working with women at all levels and being an ambassador for the fight against newborn deaths and maternal deaths, the dangers were not lost on my mind.

The constant reminders of the possible danger of pregnancy related hypertension, diabetes, preeclampsia and eclampsia were scaring me to death! Now these conditions were all possible dangers because of the age at which I got pregnant.

I lived in fear every single day, watching out for every possible sign or symptom. I constantly had panic attacks.

These were my experiences; and I'll share more details in my upcoming book on the pregnancy experience of a late bloomer. But I cried. Oh, I cried a lot during this period. My hormones were all over the place. I cried because I wished my father was alive. I cried because I was throwing up. I cried because I couldn't go out to work. I cried because…I just cried!

28

TEARS OF MOTHERHOOD

I was really looking forward to motherhood. I couldn't believe I was going to be a mother. I prepared for it in every way—or so I thought. But I didn't have the faintest idea what was coming.

I naturally like mothering and I was mothering many young people long before I had my own child and so I thought I knew 'what's up'.

Raising a child is no child's play. It is tough. And here I was. I was initially disappointed when I realized I was not carrying twins. I cried. I can't really explain my obsession with twins but I know I have always dreamt about and desired to have twins. So I was deliberate and intentional about being kind to twins and at a point, I even formed a twin club. But I think about it now and I wonder how I would have coped with twins!!

Sometimes I was simply lost. I just didn't know what to do. Let's begin from the early stages of raising a baby. I had no "older mother" to guide me initially. I had to learn and navigate the process on my own.

And of course, with the strong woman mentality, I believed I could do it all by myself if even there was nobody. So even when help came, I refused it because I wanted to do it myself. Remember I desperately wanted this child and I struggled to have her, so it was important for me to "be able", especially, since my husband had asked if I was sure I could handle and raise a baby due to my busy schedule. I so much wanted to prove capable and show him that, yes, I could and would do it.

I remember one of the ladies who came by to help got upset because, as she put it, I would not allow her to hold the baby. Sadly, to date, our relationship is strained.

I wanted to do everything for this baby myself. But the truth of the matter was that I was actually overwhelmed, only I didn't want to seem weak. As silly as it sounds now, even to me, I didn't want anyone saying or thinking they helped me take care of my baby. I wanted to have the "bragging rights" if there's any such thing. I really wanted to prove a point to 'some people'. What a shame! I cried many times from self-inflicted pain.

Though my beloved and trusted Lydia, (again if you've read Fifty Nuggets @ 50, you would know Lydia) was at hand to help, I monitored my baby like a hawk, day and night. Many people advised me, "Gifty, sleep when she sleeps and get up when she wakes up". But I didn't listen. I monitored every breath that baby took. Oh, how I wish I had listened. Now I offer the same advice but I know they don't listen because it rarely makes sense to a new mother.

And so, I was constantly overwhelmed. I was tired all the time. I had no time for anything.

Being self-employed and carrying so much in terms of responsibility, I had to go back to full time work, when she was 3 months old. A strong woman cannot let others know her vulnerability. She cannot let anyone know she needs help. This was my thinking and so I carried my burden like a "World Cup".

The real heartbreak was yet to come and it started when I resumed work.

My domestic help left at a point. I had no driver (I couldn't afford one for the job) and this meant driving with the baby in her car seat; just the two of us. I cannot describe the horror of the experience. She would cry in the middle of heavy traffic and there was no way I could make her stop crying, neither could I move out of traffic to find somewhere to park for her to feed. This often led to me breaking down in tears. I always feared our journey back home from the office because this 'mother-daughter crying contest' repeated itself every single day. It sometimes happened in the middle of the motorway, at night. Oh yes! It's been that tough.

Something that was supposed to bring me joy was now making me cry almost every day. I had mixed emotions about this whole motherhood thing.

One of my most broken phases of motherhood was in April/May 2019 when I broke my ankle and had to be in a cast for 6 weeks. I was in great pain and couldn't move without feeling the pain. But my daughter who was barely 2 years then couldn't possibly understand what was going on and always wanted to play.

The fact that I always had to raise my voice to get her to move away, coupled with her reaction to my reaction when she mistakenly touched or pushed my leg, always made me cry. "Why, mummy? Mummy, why?" and she would cry too. I share much of that experience in my books Fifty Nuggets @50 and Room 5005.

At a point, I feared I would develop postpartum depression. There was no question about the fact that I was getting depressed. I felt all alone on my motherhood journey and this led to many marital misunderstandings.

I was really struggling with handling my child alone, struggling to navigate how to take good care of her, the right things to do, yet remain successful at work. It was all too much and I cried many a tear but I would get up in the morning, dust myself of and move on to be the strength of others and impact their lives for their good.

I knew I hadn't properly dealt with the hurts, challenges and confusion that dated back to the "shock and trauma" of marriage to a traditional ruler. But I didn't realize that it was all going to eventually push me to the edge.

Yes, I was there when my husband swore the oath of allegiance, and I knew what that oath required of me, or I thought I did, until reality struck. The focus of this book is not to engage in a blame game, but to lay bare the 'cries of a strong woman'.

29

MENOPAUSE AND RAISING A TODDLER

Fast forward, I felt I had done a good job so far. At this time, she was almost 3 years old and I had hit 50. I had a few signs and symptoms of menopause, but no I didn't think menopause had anything on me—at least not yet. I was repeatedly told I didn't look 50 and a few times I doubted myself if I was indeed 50 years. I definitely didn't act like it.

However, my mood swings had escalated or risen to an uncomfortable degree. Things were really eating me up. I was going through emotions I couldn't explain. The hot flashes hit me. Feeling hot in the coolest of places. Excessive sweating. Feeling cold in the hottest of places. Body aches. Light headedness. And note: I am a woman who does her regular health checks.

I was struggling with taking care of my child. She easily irritated me and I didn't understand why, especially as she was my testimony, the gift I had prayed for and gone all out to have.

I had financial challenges; my business was struggling, I had marital issues. The world was literally closing in on me. It was getting very dark for me.

I still had to survive. Sometimes, I would leave home when my daughter had not yet woken up and by the time I got back, she would be asleep. That almost killed me! I felt as if I had failed at motherhood. Once again, a reason to cry.

That made me feel like a bad mother. Till date, I love it when I put her to sleep in my arms. But there are days I miss out on that because she may be asleep by the time I arrive home. So the times I get to put her to bed, I whisper to her 'I love you' before she goes off completely.

30

THE DARK DAYS

My dark days were getting really darker. There was this day I just suddenly screamed so loudly in the bedroom. I really screamed for no reason. I just felt like screaming. The scream was literally choking me; I had to let it out so I screamed. A few days later, I felt the same way. This time, I went outside and screamed. Another time, I went to sit in the car and again, I screamed!!!

"What is happening to me?"

Now, all this time, I was still out there, speaking on platforms to inspire and encourage people. I was having one-on-one counselling sessions with people, hosting my programmes on TV, doing my short videos of A Bit of Me, writing and bringing joy on social media, fighting for people and being a voice for the voiceless.

REMEMBER, I AM A STRONG WOMAN and strong women supposedly 'don't break down'. My foolishness.

I had a rude awakening on one of those occasions. I was going through a very rough patch in my life and couldn't sleep. I had cried my eyes out. I suddenly picked up my daughter, strapped her into her car seat and started the car, ready to drive out. Suddenly, I heard her say, "Mummy, where are we going? Don't go, mummy. No, mummy".

Her voice jolted me into reality. I checked the time and it was 2.45am. What? Where was I headed at that hour and with my daughter!!! I am shaking as I recount this incident.

I don't know the cut off point for postpartum depression but I suspect it goes beyond the first few weeks of childbirth.

My daughter started crying and I cried too. Oh, I cried so hard. I felt stupid. I felt like a failed mother. I felt like a fake who couldn't practice what she preached. I was disappointed in myself. How could I? How? What if she hadn't spoken? Would I have driven out? Where To? What if....?

Bottom line: God loves me and He saved us.

I had a conversation with one of my daughters, Dr. Emefa Klah, a medical doctor. She told me, "Mummy, you are going through your premenopausal, period!!"

"What!! So soon? But I am only 50 years." It wasn't funny!

I started reading about it and tried to manage it. In our part of the world, menopause is not a 'good thing'. People will laugh at you and even cast aspersions. Like many things that affect women, it's not talked about much, publicly.

So my strategy was to twist it to my advantage. I started referring to myself as 'menopausal' on social media. It made people laugh but I was gradually, demystifying menopause and normalizing it.

- **Covid, Menopause, Trauma and Motherhood**

Yes, COVID came with its own traumatic experiences. I still haven't recovered from the scariest period of confinement. 14 days in mandatory quarantine!

Things really got terribly low for me from the COVID period and I am still struggling to deal with all the 'bottled up and swept under the carpet' hurts, all in the name of being strong.

I managed to put together my 5th book, Broken but Beautiful, while still going through my own brokenness. I believed that as a strong woman, my mandate was bigger than my own 'wounds'. I am therefore 'a wounded healer'.

I indirectly laid bare some of my own brokenness through the many posts I made on Facebook in 2022, basically to let women know that they are not alone in their brokenness and also promote my books, especially Broken but Beautiful. But I have to say it was also my own way of venting and dealing with my challenges.

And as always, it also ended up motivating and encouraging my social media following. Sad to say though I was accused later on, of using it to 'shade' someone. You sometimes just cannot get it right no matter how hard and genuinely you try. It can get tough.

On 15th November, 2022, I posted this:

> *"I woke up this morning feeling very proud of myself!!!!*
>
> *Wow… how does she do it?*
>
> *How does Gifty Anti manage to be happy and stay happy irrespective of what she is going through and where she finds herself? How many times hasn't she been broken, yet she rises, brands and rebrands herself?*
>
> *How is she able to inspire and give of herself, even while she is bleeding inside?*
>
> *And the truth is she doesn't fake her happiness.*

Her happiness comes from deep within, I kid you not.

She appreciates every little blessing. And little things make her happy.

One moment, she is deeply sad and broken, the next, she is at her happiest best!!

Chai, it's a mystery to me and I think it's a course that must be studied at the PhD level. You think you know my story? You don't even know 1/100th of my story and my journey. But so long as God lives, I am unstoppable. Today, I pray that you find genuine happiness that comes from deep within you. The happiness that only you can give you".

Interestingly, that was the day November 15, 2022 happened. Well, that's for another day. I also posted this in early November.

"To the one hurting, disappointed and going through some form of brokenness... I know it doesn't look like it now... But believe me, you will be fine.
Things will fall into pleasant places for you.
Just hold on and trust God!!
Your 'One Day' will soon come.
You will laugh again. You will dance again.
Till then, take it one day at a time."

I posted it, but I had no idea what was coming my way. I didn't know my life and that of my daughter, were going to be shaken beyond anything we had ever gone through. I didn't know that post was my inner being talking to me because of what was to come.

November 15, 2022 happened to us.

There is nothing as painful as a woman raising a child while trying to heal from her inner wounds. You will be screaming loudly inside and with tears in your eyes, but still hold it together for the sake of your child.

I remember days when my little girl could sense my inner struggles and ask, "Mummy, what is wrong?"

Especially, after November 15, 2022, she could sense something was wrong but didn't understand what it was. She would sometimes take the phone away from me and tell me to stop talking to people because they are making me cry. Bless her little heart.

So many rumors were flying around, but I just couldn't defend myself. That I have been able to put myself together to even write this book is the doing of the Lord.

31

THE OPTIONS

One thing about a strong woman dealing with fear, hurt, failures and betrayal is that she lives in denial till she breaks down one day.

And this is the process she often goes through.

1. She first lives in denial, constantly telling herself she is strong. She can handle this. Yes, she is strong.

2. Then she cries her heart out. Still keeping things to herself.

3. Then she blames herself for letting that happen to her. "I am Gifty Naana Afia Dansoa Anti, the most celebrated female media personality with over 60 awards and hundreds of citations. The woman with super crazy faith in God. How can this happen to me? How could I let this happen

to me? I should have known better!"

4. Then she doubts herself. "Is there something I should have done and didn't do? Or did I do something I shouldn't have done?" This stage can drain her and deprive her of her self-worth and confidence.

5. And when the healing process seems to take forever, she will get angry with herself. The frustration can push her into depression and she will second guess herself until she fully heals and then picks herself up and moves on.

It can be a long and very lonely journey. Lord help us.

32

THE BREAKING NEWS

"Well, don't be sad or disappointed but currently..." I then told the group of 10 ladies, about November 15, 2022.

The room went dead silent. Most of them were speechless, mouths open with tears in their eyes but unable to say anything. It was obvious some had already heard it but didn't know how to ask me. They weren't sure if it was true, because I looked and acted like the strong woman I had always been.

I am so grateful to God and so proud of how far I have come, and how I have been able to hold and keep my life together. It is all by the Grace of God because the tears I have cried since November 15, 2022, could eradicate desertification. It is not just because it happened, but how it came about and what happened prior to and afterwards. The realization that supposed allies were, in fact, my detractors.

But I know I will heal. Maybe not today, maybe not tomorrow or next week or next month… but I will heal. It is only a matter of time.

So my dear strong woman, we all do go through our crying moments and different experiences make us cry. It's perfectly OK.

It's perfectly OK to accept that as a strong woman, you can be and feel vulnerable and miserable sometimes; that you feel weak, broken, lost, confused and totally fed up sometimes. It's even OK to feel like giving up sometimes. It's OK. But it's not OK to actually give up. No, don't!!!

I am sure you are wondering how I was able to deal with all this and still keep going. How was I able to make it seem as if all was well? How could I have been dealing with our separation on November 15, 2022 and still carry on as if nothing had happened? Looking happy and in charge on social media and mounting great platforms and speaking at programmes?

No, I didn't fake it. No, I am not the type that pretends.

I cried. Oh, I cried many times. I felt like giving up. It affected me in many ways and many times I shut off. Especially, when my daughter would ask me questions I had no answers to. But I found coping strategies.

Thankfully, I have come to understand that sometimes, you can actually "GIVE WHAT YOU DON'T HAVE". You may not have peace, but you can give others peace. You may not have joy, but you can give others joy. You may not have money, but you can point out to people how to work towards their goal. I have come to understand, that for most of us the strong women, our mission is greater than us. It is not about us. We don't and can't have the luxury of giving up because of our personal circumstances. No, we can't.

I am grateful to Pastor Ruth Tiso, a Baptist priest based in London and Mrs Kuukua Maurice Ankrah, a lawyer, entrepreneur and woman of God in her own right, for literally holding my hand during these darkest of days. They are both strong women who have had and still have their own crying moments. But they understand "the assignment" and they carry it faithfully.

As for my "let me be brutally honest with you Gifty", sister, Emma Ampofo (if you have read any of my books, you know who she is), I can't thank her enough. I often 'run' away from her because the honest truth hurts sometimes. But the best friend/ sister anyone can ever have, is the one who can be brutally honest with you. I love her to bits.

I am grateful to my God-ordained twins, Jenny and Jennifer of Twinnie Krafts, for coming into my life at the time they did. They bombarded me with prayers.

I am also grateful to my siblings and my family for holding me up and standing with me in these times.

So yes, I am a strong, resilient woman. A woman with super crazy faith in God. One moment, I am speaking to thousands of people and the next I am speaking to only 10 people in a room. I know I am called to be 'a national and international champion', but I have never been afraid to be 'a local champion'. I have travelled to many countries outside Ghana as a professional, but so have I travelled to many towns and villages in Ghana. I often smile and many people have referred to me as their inspiration.

But yes, I cry too, and I am not afraid to admit that I have my moments of weakness and brokenness, moments of wishing to give up.

Bottom line, ladies: we need each other. We need to create safe spaces where we can detox, freely talk and share our hurts, pains, fears, desires and even our confessions without feeling anxious about being judged or sold out.

We need detox avenues. And as you read this book, can you offer yourself up to be a woman another woman can trust?

I don't know what makes you cry, my dear strong woman. Maybe your experience hasn't been mentioned in this book, but at least you know that you are not the only one who cries. I also want you to know that it's OK if you want to cry only "in the shower or rain". But it is also very OK if you have to cry publicly, openly and freely. It's OK to tell and share your story with the world. Silence is not always golden. Keeping it all in can 'kill' you.

At the appropriate time, I shall write fully about November 15, but for now, I give you the One who has and still holds my head high. I give you Jesus. I give you the Holy Spirit. I give you God.

It is a shame that we have been socialised to believe that a strong woman must only cry in the rain, if at all. It's a great shame because it need not be so.

A woman, especially, a strong woman, will always be hit by circumstances that will make her cry; the worst of all, probably being the shocking realization that her detractors are closer than she could ever imagine. But, there will always be detractors; that is just life. However, the strong Woman who knows God, will forever stay strong.

Dear strong woman, keep lifting your head high. Keep going, keep pushing. Never give up on yourself. Once you have life, there is nothing you cannot achieve.

Make the best out of every situation life throws your way. Your purpose, mission, vision and ministry are bigger than you see.

Cry whenever you feel like it; cry freely. But always rise up in the morning, pray, dress up, show up and like Esther, trust God to fulfil His promise concerning you.

STAY STRONG.

Conclusion

THE AGONY OF A STRONG WOMAN

About two weeks before the launch of this book, I thought of changing the title from When Strong Women Cry to The Agony of A Strong Woman. But I decided against it because that could be a new book, perhaps a sequel to this one.

On 19th April 2023, the early childhood program of my daughter's school had a sporting day which they call Blue and White Day. As usual, I went there and my husband joined me later. He had to go to the hospital before joining me because he was unwell.

After the program, I had many Whatsapp messages asking me what was going on in my marriage. I was confused. Then they started sending me screenshots of posts by bloggers and social media postings on my husband and me.

Posts accused me of 'Sacking my husband' from my house. Initially, I laughed because whoever is giving them the information had it twisted. But it got worse. I couldn't sleep that whole night. I had calls and messages from all over the world. Some accused me of being wicked without finding out whether the stories were true or not. Others were hailing me for "avenging them" because they had been thrown out of their homes by their husbands. It was a tough night.

The following day 20th April was worse. The social media headlines accused me of maltreating my husband, disrespecting him, locking him outside whenever her went out and the most ridiculous one was that his side chic had come to the house with a baby and I kicked both of them out. How can people just be so mean? Just cook up stories.. just to destroy someone. For what reason? What do they get out of it?

It was heartbreaking and embarrassing. The insults, insinuations, accusations, falsehood, ridicule…. I suffered it all. But my husband was sick and so I had to be strong for me and him and my little girl too.

God knows why these attacks had to come at the time my husband was sick. Because the feisty side of me would have had serious confrontations with him. Accusing him of letting me go through all these. But God knows I will still fight with him when he gets well.

It was bad timing but God works in mysterious ways and His ways are not our ways.

Yes, we had been talking and trying to fix our differences but this incident of social media attacks and falsehoods made us realize that we needed each other and have to try our best to make things work. So help us, God.

We saw those who were for us and those against us. I kept my cool throughout the period and didn't react despite the provocations. It was tough and I cried for many days.

I remember on the morning of 20th April when I dropped off my daughter at school, I joined the Car Park Congress (a group of parents who meet up at the car park of Association international school after we drop off our children for a little chitchat on everything and anything). They all gave me a huge hug and I just broke down and cried out. The tears I was holding back, finally came gushing out. It was a safe space to let it all out.

Yes, like most marriages, we had our issues. And no I didn't kick my husband out of the house. I never locked him outside, I didn't disrespect him knowingly or deliberately and no side chic brought a child to our home.

Those behind these attacks (whoever they are), meant it for evil, but God used it to bring my husband and me together, closer than before. The process would have been a bit longer, but God used this painful experience (embarrassment, insults, etc hurled at me) and my husband being sick (as awkward as it may sound) to hasten the process of us reconciling our differences.

It is my prayer, that God will use this book to also hasten unto you, your HEALING!!

Recommendations: OGA's Take

To the strong woman crying, you are not alone.

Anything that makes you cry not out of joy or excitement, is causing you pain and you must deal with it. It is important to heal from this pain. It may take a long time, but you must heal. One day at a time.

Your pain and how you handle it has a voice and speaks volumes. Let it speak to you and to others.

Here are some 10 strategies I recommend

1. First of all, it's OK to accept that you are but human. You can't have it all 'perfectly done'. No. You may be good, actually excellent at 3 or 4 things but fail at one or two things and it's perfectly OK. Don't be too hard on yourself. You are not superwoman. Even superwoman who exists only in movies has days when she is

defeated.

Like Naomi in the Bible, it is sometimes good, actually important, to move from the 'place' that has or is causing you pain. It is necessary to move away from there for your own health and sanity.

There is an Akan saying that you can't stay in an ant infested place and try to get the ants off you. It is very difficult to stay in a place of pain and heal. It is difficult. And it is sometimes best to move away and never look back. It is going to be a tough and lonely road but it gets better. Trust me. It gets better with time and there will be a time when you will actually look back and smile or laugh.

But never regret the experience, because depending on how you react to it, it will either make you better or bitter. And I pray it makes you better.

2. It is also sometimes important to 'breathe'. Take a break and reassess the situation. What you did wrong and where you got it wrong.

It is important to accept that maybe you over stressed yourself, took things for granted or overly did things. This is not to blame yourself but to accept that you are only human and you make mistakes. Learn to forgive yourself.

The "15th November. 2023" period of my life was

tough. Really tough in the beginning because of who we are in society. The talk, the fears, the boomerang effect, if it should come out.

But after 5 months, we both realized that there was more at stake than the 2 of us and our daughter; and so we had to talk to find the way 'back in or out'.

I also understood why our mothers stayed in toxic marriages because of us, their children. Some women of today also stay in abusive marriages because of their children. I do not endorse this strategy. They did not know of any other strategy or way out. Everyone around them told them the same thing: Endure for the sake of the child. Oh, how they may have died inside each day.

No reason is good enough for a woman to stay in a toxic relationship, especially, if her mental health and life are at stake. No. No matter how dire the consequences may be, you need to be alive and sane for your own sake and for the sake of the children. You need to put yourself first and that's perfectly OK.

Your value is way weightier than marriage.

My daughter was, perhaps, the hardest hit in this separation. She would consistently ask me questions I could not answer because I didn't want to lie to her or give her false hope. I also didn't think that at 5 years, she would understand what was going on if I had told her. She would prevent me from sleeping at her father's side of the bed because "Daddy will soon come home". She would also cry and tell me to "call Daddy and ask him to come back". She became clingy and consistently asked me 'mummy are you going to leave me too".

It was tough. But that was not the reason we talked about the way forward. I knew she would get over it at some point. But I had to tread cautiously.

One of the things that women going through separation or divorce have to guard against is how they treat the children. How they vent to them. How they tell them their side of the story without trying to make them hate their father, no matter how much he has hurt them. Let the children make their own decisions on how to react to the situation. Again, I say it is tough.

If they are little, mind how you make them see you. You need to be strong for them. Don't let them see you sad or cry all the time. It affects them negatively and it will reflect in their academic performance and later developments.

If they are old enough, that is, 18 years and above, it's OK to let them see you break down and vulnerable. But let them see you pick yourself up every day and move you. Take them along your healing journey. The ups and downs, so they learn early that it's OK to cry as a strong woman. That way, they will know that there will things that will break them in life, but they should pick themselves up.

3. There is a conversation that ' strong women' need to have, especially about how we raise our boys and how we build a relationship with the men who come into our lives.

    Let's raise our boys to be responsible human beings. Let's raise them to embrace girls, females, women as partners in all aspects of life. Not their servants or lesser human beings that they have to dominate in order to feel their masculine powers and energy. It's not an ego contest. Let us educate, raise and empower them to understand that being the ' head of the family' does not make you 'a lord and savior'. They must understand from an early age that the woman is not his competitor or his enemy of progress but partner for a successful journey of life.

    Raise them to appreciate what strong women do for them and not to have a sense of entitlement.

    And when it comes to the men we marry or date, let us stop making them feel entitled by encouraging them to be 'irresponsible'.

Sometimes, in an attempt to make the men know and see us as strong and capable women, we turn to do things or take charge of things that are not our responsibility. Sometimes, we tend to 'change the men' to suit our 'taste' by doing almost everything thing for them and then it becomes a standard that we have to maintain, without they wanting to lift a finger. Because after all, they didn't ask for it, we gave it to them on a silver platter.

There are things I have done for men that I would tell my younger self never to do. I never, me fixing and pimping up the house of a man I was dating so I could feel comfortable there whenever I visited. Meanwhile, I was going there only once a while and the longest period of time I stayed over was a weekend. Go there on Friday after work and leave Sunday morning. Oh my! Girls have done foolish things. But it's all good. It's an experience.

Some men would appreciate and catch up fast and take charge of 'that responsibility', understanding that you are only trying to help them. But sometimes, it makes some men develop a sense of entitlement and expect you as a woman to do everything, because as it was in the beginning—how you started it, you will do it if he doesn't. After all, you are a strong woman.

If you are in such a situation, it is not too late to pause, have a conversation with this man and let him know that you were only helping and it is time for him to step up and take charge of his own life.

You need to have tough conversations with yourself and ask what ifs?

4. No woman is indispensable. Not one. But there are women who are unforgettable and irreplaceable.

   Be that woman. Always add value to yourself. Consistently brand and rebrand yourself. Your mystery, power and asset are your confidence, boldness, intelligence and taking calculated risks. Be articulate and clear in speech. Be original. Let them take you as you are but be prepared to make adjusts and compromises that will not 'harm' you or your brand, for the greater good.

   Learn to tell people the hard truths to their face, without 'damaging them'. Be tactful with your words. Be genuine. Always bounce back no matter how hard life treats you. Understand that it takes time and that life happens.

   Know that you can rise above even shame or disgrace. Let society—or whoever talk. But know that you are not the first and you won't be the last.

The best form of revenge, is to succeed.

5. To the feminist/gender activist/advocate, note that it can get so exhausting and heart breaking to see and hear the things you have fought against or empowered women against repeating themselves. It is difficult to feel used by some women to fight for their causes only for them to turn against you. It is tough.

Be kind to yourself. Understand that you can't save everyone. You can't rescue everybody. Look back and around you and solidify the gains you have made.

Learn to take breaks to work on yourself and your family. Learn to turn off the noises, especially on social and mainstream media that churn out patriarchal and misogynistic theories that seek to make nonsense of our cause.

One of the things that used to break me was when anti-feminists taunted and trolled me for getting married. It used to make me angry and sometimes made me regret marrying, especially when things became shaky in the marriage.

But I know better now. I know these are deliberate and calculated attempts by them to break me, silence me and make the younger ones who look up to me sell their souls to the devil by losing faith and trust in the feminism agenda.

I remember quite recently when I said "men are afraid of strong women", (a statement I still stand by), my husband was trolled and teased as being 'afraid man'. To wit, he is afraid of me that's why I made that statement. He never said anything about it but I won't be surprised if it affected him somehow, but typically of him, he took it in his stride.

My big sister also told me recently about people sending them screenshots of things I say and what people say about me on social media and how it affects them—my siblings. So I took my time to explain to her what I stand for, what I seek to achieve and the implications of my activism. It doesn't make it any easier for them, but at least, they now know that I know what I am doing.

It is important for us to have such conversations with our family and our loved ones, because they also do get affected, no matter how proud they are of us.

Feminism is also about choices. You can chose to marry or not to marry. To have children or not to have children. As a feminist, it is OK to want things that makes you feel like 'a woman'. It's OK.

It's your choice. So long as you don't feel less as a woman because you don't have those things, you are good.

 So yes, they will continue to insult us, insinuate things and even troll us. But do you believe in the cause? How passionate are you about it? How much and how many 'hits' are you willing to take for the sake of the feminists agenda?

Some women have stopped calling themselves feminists, all because of what the anti-feminists have continuously thrown at them and their families. And sometimes, these have dire effects on them and their families and so they relinquish the tag. It is also OK. It's their choice.

Of course, there are extremisms in every cause in society. And so every now and then it's OK to pause and reassess, rejuvenate, revive and renew your strategy.

But if you believe in the cause, I urge you to keep pushing the gender agenda.

6. As a strong woman, find safe spaces to talk and vent. Spaces where you can let it all out without fearing that your secrets will be used against you in the nearest future.

   Don't be afraid to speak with clinical psychologists or counselors if your mental health is at stake.

And oh, mental health disorders among women is on the increase now, all because we are bottling up things, all in the name of strong women must not have weaknesses or make mistakes.

I know most of us have had bad experiences with sharing our challenges with other women and they have let us down big time, so you can choose to go to a professional.

However, nothing beats having your tribe of women with whom you can share freely your deepest pains and fears.

Fear is one of the cancers that actually destroys strong women. Keeping up appearances.

 Don't be afraid to try again. Don't. This time, you have the benefit of experience so you will or must be cautious. But by all means, try again if you want to. You may cry again and so what? We all cry. Both rich and poor. Male and female. Young and old. So please, dare to try again.

Learn to go through the process of healing. Be kind to yourself often. Take time out to rejuvenate.

You deserve to be happy. You deserve the good and finest things in life. You deserve it amen and if you can afford it, go for it.

And dare to be there for another woman. Dare to

hold the hands of another woman going through what you have been through. Let her understand that she is not the first and can't be the last.

7. Sometimes, we heal fastest when we help others go through their pain regardless of our pain.

   Turning your pain into power is always an important strategy. After losing Nicole, her daughter to cancer, Gloria Abla Pwamang decided to channel her energy towards helping other families with children who have cancer, through a he Woesomo Foundation.

   Mary Amoah set up a center to train and help other parents who have children with autism.

   Many others have done same and become more powerful and influential in society because they decided to let their messes be a message that will transform others.

   Do not give up on yourself, family and loved ones because of your pain.

   Do not let those tears go wasted. They are precious. Let something good come out of them.

8. It is also important to sometimes go back to your 'first love'. There are many of us who abandoned our dreams and aspirations for one reason or the other.

Sometimes when 'affliction' strikes, it's important to go back to that dream. Go back to school to pursue that course. Learn that trade or skill. Learn that sport or game. It helps in the healing process.

Lose that weight you've always wanted to, for yourself. Change that hair style, dressing and sometimes even that job.

I had always known I wanted to be an author. I procrastinated until I was 'afflicted' and I took that phone and started writing.

Little changes also go a long way to help your wipe your 'tears'.

9. A strong woman must be intentional in the decisions and actions she takes, and the choices she makes as she strives to heal from what makes her cry. They must be calculated.

   It will not be easy,and it may defy all that you have believed in over the years. But it may be what you need to do to end the crying.

   It may take making sacrifices that you had sworn you will never make. It may sometimes mean going against your 'principled' position you have taken. Justified as it may be. It may mean moving out of your comfort zone and depriving you of what you believe you deserve.

I remember when I had to leave a relationship I had spent 10 years in. I wrote about it in my book 50 Nuggets @ 50. I had to let go of the things I felt I deserved because of what I had endured and contributed to the relationship. But I realized that holding on to that was going to tie me and constantly link me to the very thing that was making me crying.

Leaving my former employment, GBC, was the same. It was scary. I didn't know what the future held, how I was going to survive without a monthly pay. But I took a bold step, because the crying had to stop. This is a story for another book.

And quite recently, I had sworn I was not going to go to Adumasa for Easter 2023 and I had justified to everyone who tried to persuade me to go why I can't go.

Even the woman I had never said no to, the woman whose counsel I have always believed in and which has often worked for me, Nana Afrakoma II, Paramount Queenmother of Akwamu Traditional Area, decided not to say anything again.

But when I had that dream and saw the children looking down at me and crying and hearing a voice ask me, "Are you going to deprive these children, yourself and those who support you, of their blessings, all because of your pain?" I knew I had to push aside my pain, pride and prejudice to go and put smiles on the faces of the little ones and the aged at Adumasa. Especially when I had the same dream twice in less than 24 hours.

It wasn't easy. I even felt God was not being fair to me. Asking me to go back to the very place where I have cried. The very place where I felt disrespected and taken for granted.

But the Holy Spirit reminded me of Moses. God sent Moses back to the very place where he had to run from.

Not only did I find joy in the act of giving to the little ones and the aged, thanks to the support I received in my 3 day appeal for support, I was also honoured by the Youth of Adumasa, for my contribution towards the development of the town and for inspiring them to believe in the future of their town, proving that no matter the number of people who pretend not to see your worth or who disrespect you, there are many others who appreciate, respect and value your worth.

So be intentional. Against all odds, take that step; it might be the very thing that will help your healing, or help you regain your confidence and self-worth and remind you of who you are: a good human being, strong, powerful and influential.

For you, the call may not be a dream or the Holy spiritual. It may be an instinct. Strong enough to make you uncomfortable in your spirit. But be intentional about obeying it.

Sometimes, you may have to talk to or go back to the person you have sworn never to reopen links or communication with.

You have the right to change your mind and people change to become better or worse. You may never know.

10. Let me add this, prayer is a therapy. It is a very powerful therapeutic strategy. Learn to pray through your challenges. Learn to cry on God. Learn to let it all out in prayer.

    And note this, prayer is not only when you shout, spit out fire and 'blast in tongues'. Prayer is also that silent cry and conversations in your head focusing on God. Prayer is singing or listening to that worship song and soaking it all in. Praying is dancing before the Lord.

    Have faith that God will give you strength to go through the process of healing. Remember, "Come to me, ye that are laboured and heavily burdened," says the Lord. And "Yeah, though I go through the valley of the shadow of death, I will fear no evil".

God is always your ultimate plug when you want strength to heal. When you want that miracle. When you need a testimony.

And learn to also trust God's perfect will for your life.

Take a step of boldness backed by prayer.

Esther stepped out to appear before the King, knowing that she could 'perish'. She prayed and fasted and then took that step of faith for the sake of her uncle and her people.

Abigail prayed and dared to step out to meet David and his men, to appeal and plead with him to spare her household, knowing very well she was married to a wicked man.

Deborah prayed and stepped up to tell Barak, the army general what the Lord had told her, and took another bold step to go to war with them.

Ruth took that bold step to go with Naomi to an unknown land to try again.

The strongest among us is the one who knows and trusts God.

What OGA Has Going On Now

I have availed myself to speak to groups, churches, schools, etc., on any issues concerning women, the youth and young ones.

I have done this for over 15 years.

You can book me for any speaking engagements on 0203535500, 0208861919 or 0543618182.

I have also started a detox programme known as Conversations with Gifty Anti.

This is a safe space where small groups of women, 50 at a time, come together and share, vent and get counsel. No phones allowed and no recordings allowed.

It is a paid-for event and the first one was held on 13th February, 2023, with young women in the media.

I also organise retreats for a get-away fun time to detox mentally and physically.

To book or register,   call or WhatsApp 0203525500, 0208861919 or 0543618182.

Follow me on all my social media handles for upcoming events and updates.

 Oheneyere Gifty Anti - OGA
 oheneyere_gifty_anti

Feedback From The Detox Session

"After the session, I also made myself available for another strong woman to cry. She had lost her mum, and now, unfortunately, I also know the feeling of losing a very dear one. That space gave her the opportunity to cry, laugh, and even advise me. But it was a real detox for her.

Mama, this was how powerful that session we had with you was for me. Because I got to detox, I was in a much better place to help another detox.

Only God knows how much healing this book will bring to 1000s if I am not exaggerating. God dey, so we dey."

—Eugenia Boadi

"Thank you for inviting me to meet your children. They are great and I'm happy you have women who love and support you.

I was a little sad though because I didn't know you had people who dislike you for the help and support you give. I was shocked.

Do you 'Dee', (she calls me Dee) you always have God and me to fall back on.

It's your calling.

The world is a better place with you in it.

You, me, always."

—Babiee Dappah

"As women in the activism space, dedicated to being the voice of the voiceless; fighting tirelessly for others around us, lending our strength to others… it can be hard for us to break down. To vent. To cry.

Because who can we turn to? We're the "strong ones," the "keyboard gangsters," the "magajias."And if we break down, we with our privilege and voice and stature, who can mend our pieces?

Who heals the healer?

Who guards the guardian?

That detox session was a joy and a gift and I learnt

two important lessons:

1. I can eat two different kinds of kenkey in one sitting

2. I am not alone on this journey; I have a small army of intelligent, wise, loving, passionate, vivacious women surrounding me.

Activism is hard work and I'm learning how to take breaks and pace myself. I'm learning how to erect boundaries and keep them firmly in place. I'm unlearning the notion that I have to be strong and infallible and indefatigable.

I'm learning how to move in my power and not be beholden to what society says about me because people will say what they want to say anyway.

Every activist needs a safe space and our detox session with our Mama G showed me that those women...that army of intelligent, wise, loving, passionate, vivacious—to-give women... are my safe space."

—Jayjay Akuamoah

As a feminist activist with chronic illness, I have experienced my fair share of struggles and challenges in fighting for the causes that matter to me. Balancing my health needs with my activist work has been a constant juggling act, and there have been times when my illness has made it difficult to participate in events or take on new projects. However, I have found that my experiences with chronic illness have also given me a unique perspective on the issues that I care about and have motivated me to continue fighting for change.

One of the most transformative experiences I have had as a young feminist activist was participating in the detox session with a group of fellow feminist activists. It was a chance for us to unpack and share our experiences in a safe space, and to gain insight and understanding into the struggles we face as activists. I made a strategic choice to wear a maternity outfit, which allowed me to o fully enjoy the Kenkey and all the accompanying protein it had to offer lol without worrying about any discomfort.

During the session, we were able to break down harmful clichés about women being their enemies, and instead come together to support each other as Mama's avengers. This experience reinforced the notion that it's okay for even strong women to show vulnerability, and it was truly comforting to feel a sense of camaraderie and shared experience in that safe space.

Through my work as a feminist activist, I have been able to design and implement programs that have impacted the lives of over 20,000 women, children, persons living with disabilities, and other minority groups in Ghana. These programs focus on a range of issues, including sexual and Gender-Based violence, sexual reproductive health rights, girls' mentorship, economic livelihood empowerment, and women in leadership.

Despite the challenges of living with chronic illness, activism has given me an outlet to share my experiences, advocate for changes, and connect with others who are also dealing with chronic illness. I have used my experiences to raise awareness about the realities of living with chronic illness and to call for better access to healthcare services for those who need them.

It's important to remember that even the strongest and most resilient individuals need to take a moment to pause and process their emotions. As a feminist activist with chronic illness, it can be especially challenging to balance self-care with activism work. However, I am determined to continue advocating for gender equality, social justice, and human rights for all.

I know that there are many others out there who are also fighting for the same causes, and together we can make a real difference. We need to support each other and create safe spaces where we can share our experiences and offer each other encouragement and support. Let's continue to work towards a more inclusive and understanding world, one step at a time.

I am proud to have been a part of this powerful and transformative experience, and Dear Gifty, I'm deeply grateful for the trust placed in me to share your profound personal experiences that many activists from previous generations would never have disclosed. Thank you!

—Franka Nancy Hagan, Short Avenger

Other Books By The Author